REINVENTING JAPAN

INTERNATIONAL MIGRATION SERIES

REINVENTING JAPAN

IMMIGRATION'S ROLE
IN SHAPING JAPAN'S FUTURE

DEMETRIOS G. PAPADEMETRIOU
KIMBERLY A. HAMILTON

CARNEGIE ENDOWMENT FOR INTERNATIONAL PEACE
WASHINGTON, D.C.

To order *Reinventing Japan: Immigration's Role in Shaping Japan's Future* contact Carnegie's distributor, The Brookings Institution Press Department 029, Washington, D.C. 20042-0029, USA
1-800-275-1447 or 1-202-797-6258
Fax 202-797-6004, Email bibooks@brook.edu

Library of Congress Cataloging-in-Publication Data

Papademetriou, Demetrios G., 1946-
  Reinventing Japan : immigration's role in shaping Japan's future / by Demetrios G. Papademetriou and Kimberly A. Hamilton.
    p. cm. — (International migration policy program ; 10)
Includes bibliographical references and index.
  ISBN 0-87003-182-1 pbk.
    1. Japan—Emigration and immigration—Government policy. I. Hamilton, Kimberly A. II. Title. III. International Migration Policy Program (Series) ; 10.
JV8723 .P36 2000
325.52'09'049—dc21

                                                                00-010227

Edited by Linda J. Lotz
Design by Paddy McLaughlin Concepts & Design

CONTENTS

TABLES AND FIGURES

TABLES

FIGURES

PREFACE

mmigration is taking on new importance in industrial-ized countries. Whether because of labor shortages brought on by a booming economy, as in the United States, or because of perceived threats to national security and social and political order, as in the European Union, the industrial world's politicians and policy makers are now paying much closer attention to the issue of international migration. One emerging factor—the aging of these societies' populations—will force those industrialized countries most skeptical about the economic value and political viability of immigration to reevaluate their approach. With the populations of most industrialized countries rapidly growing older, the prospects of shrinking labor forces and a concomitant erosion of the tax base are expected to compel policy makers to reconsider their views about immigration, with an eye to assessing its role in addressing these demographic realities.

Nowhere are these pressures stronger than in Japan, where total fertility rates have been among the lowest in the world for several decades. This demographic epiphany, coupled with Japanese workers' increasing unwillingness to take the lowest-skilled jobs, has translated into a growing reliance on immigrants of different skills and statuses—including illegals. That reliance, however, remains officially unacknowledged. As a result, Japan continues to seek and find comfort in its social and cultural "exceptionalism" and remains suspicious of outsiders, a tendency that translates into restrictive immigration policies.

Can Japan reconcile demographically induced economic realities with concerns about social instability and the feared dilution of its culture? How might it do so? These are the central questions that immigration poses not only for Japan but for all industrialized countries. What makes Japan most interesting as a case study is that nowhere else in the world is this question posed more starkly. In the next decade, Japan will have the greatest need for more open immigration policies. Japanese politicians and policy makers are also likely to encounter the greatest social resistance to such a course. This monograph deals with this struggle between economic realism, on the one hand, and the sense that the uniqueness of Japanese society and culture must be defended against the presumed "onslaught" of foreign immigrants, on the other. We call on

Japanese leaders to address this question head-on, and although we do not offer a detailed prescription (this is a conversation that the Japanese must have), we provide the analysis and offer general guidelines for thinking about possible answers.

This text would not have been possible without the help of others. The authors would like to thank Chikako Kashiwazaki and Yasushi Iguchi for their indispensable support as readers and commentators; Nikhilesh Mohan Korgaonkar for his research assistance; and Amelia Brown for providing valuable updates, producing the tables and graphs, and shepherding this manuscript to its completion. It would be fair to say that this essay could not have been produced without her tireless efforts and her attention to detail.

INTRODUCTION

s the twenty-first century dawns, Japan finds itself once again entering uncharted waters. Navigating between tradition and modernity, Japan is weighing whether to jettison a broad range of cherished social and cultural values in order to stay the economic course. Oddly, it is the same international economic system that Japan has learned to negotiate and profit from so masterfully that is demanding that Japan either adapt to the changing requirements of the international political economy or take its place in the second tier of politically—and economically—influential powers.

What will Japan do? Following two decades of nearly uninterrupted economic expansion, Japan was in the grasp of persistent recession and wrenching restructuring for most of the 1990s. These forces are now combining with the social and economic implications of Japan's demographic realities to cut to the heart of Japanese collective identity and to cast doubt on Japan's economic future. The stakes are high. Will the world's second largest economy and its largest *net* exporter[1] engage deeply enough in what the late Joseph Schumpeter called "creative destruction" to maintain its leading global position and enhance its dominant position in Asia? Will this moment, being heralded by some as Japan's "third opening,"[2] be able to match the dramatic transfor-

---

[1] However, Japan is also the country with the heaviest debt burden among advanced industrial societies.

[2] Ichiro Ozawa (former president of Japan's largest opposition party in the mid-1990s, the New Frontier Party) points out that the "first opening" occurred in the mid-nineteenth century with the introduction of liberal political and economic values during the

mations of the Meiji Restoration and the post–World War II period and thus replicate their effects on Japanese growth and prosperity? Put somewhat differently, will Japan's social and political institutions prove, once again, equal to managing the challenges such change implies? And finally, will the Japanese social and political fabric tolerate the depth of change this new opening will require?

In this essay we explore primarily one aspect[3]—albeit an essential one—of the changes necessary for Japan to remain a principal global economic and political player: opening itself to legal and *increasingly permanent* immigration. So far, Japan has resisted a significant opening in these policy fields despite an economy that was, until recently, robust; labor shortages that, in the late 1980s and early 1990s, led to job openings regularly outnumbering job applicants; and, since 1995, a *shrinking* workforce. Indeed, despite current concerns about unemployment, Japan must now begin to educate the public about the proper place for immigrants in its long-term economic and social future. The policy outcome of this effort will have an enormous influence on Japan's long-term economic competitiveness. And if Japan does open itself up to immigrants, the decision will form the basis of a radical metamorphosis of one of the most homogeneous yet economically successful global actors.

Historically, Japan has been a relatively closed society and has used virtually every conceivable means in its policy arsenal to defer either directly or indirectly a decision in favor of a significant loosening in its immigration policies. To this end, Japan has relied

---

Meiji era, including the establishment of universal education, constitutional democracy, and capitalism. These values were reemphasized during the "second opening"—the period of American occupation after the Second World War—when voting rights were extended to women, landholding laws were reformed, and labor rights began to take hold. The changes that took place during these radical times of change, Ozawa contends, allowed Japan to grow into the power it has become. Now, Ozawa argues, Japan must engage the international community anew and adopt a new receptivity toward ideas and people from other cultures. Failing to do so may condemn Japan to falling behind in the twenty-first century (Ozawa 1996).

[3]Other changes facing Japan include opening its markets much more widely to foreign products, finishing the much-needed banking reforms it has undertaken in recent years (sometimes haltingly and often incompletely), and pursuing in a meaningful way the economic and labor market reforms it is beginning to make. These and related reforms are threatened by Japan's consensus-seeking policy-making model, which reinforces the bureaucratic inertia that is the enemy of all fundamental change. For these reforms to move forward and take hold, greater and more sustained political leadership will be required.

on three broad strategies with varying degrees of steadfastness and with limited success.

The first strategy has been built around Japan's methodical pursuit of foreign direct investment (FDI). FDI is, first and foremost, an international *economic* strategy—intended to capture both emerging and mature markets and to inoculate producers against the vagaries of import controls. For Japan, however, FDI has also served as a means of "exporting" large numbers of production and assembly jobs, thus providing some relief from labor shortages in Japan. Such investments, especially those focusing in Asia, have also had another—in some ways fortuitous—effect: they have created a large number of jobs in the region, which in turn may have mitigated some of the regional immigration pressures on Japan. Although this appears to be more of an afterthought than a coordinated policy, it has given the Japanese government some leverage in its pursuit of cooperation from other countries in the region in the management of unwanted migration.

The second strategy has involved a limited opening in Japan's immigration system. In 1990, Japan enacted an extensive set of amendments to its 1951 immigration law. These changes broadened admissions categories to include most forms of temporary immigration categories from the U.S. "nonimmigrant" (that is, temporary migrant) classification system. The 1990 changes also allowed persons of Japanese descent living outside of Japan (*Nikkeijin*) to immigrate to Japan, offered additional rights to foreign-born spouses and children of Japanese nationals, and altered and expanded the foreign trainee program (which brings foreigners to Japan for job training).

The limited opening in Japan's immigration system has helped address some of Japan's labor needs while also demonstrating, in a small way, Japan's capacity to adapt to economic imperatives. The broadening of temporary admissions categories has promoted the immigration of skilled foreign workers, helping Japan accrue and benefit from international talent in a variety of fields and keeping the global component of the Japanese economy humming. Furthermore, permitting the entry of certain categories of unskilled workers—namely, *Nikkeijin* and trainees—has added badly needed if grossly inadequate numbers to the workforce. Finally, opening up the immigration system so that it is more reciprocal toward Japan's economic partners fulfills not only an eco-

3

nomic need but also Japan's obligations under the international trading regime from which it has benefited so handsomely.[4]

The third and final strategy goes to the very heart of the global migration system. A substantial number of foreign workers—estimated at 300,000 to 500,000 for most of the 1990s—have been "allowed" to work without formal authorization in a variety of secondary labor markets and the underground economy. Such workers, most of whom enter legally but violate the terms of their visas, remain in Japan for extended periods. Critics of Japanese immigration policy view the presence of these workers as an unacknowledged concession by the government to those economic sectors squeezed by Japan's opening to the global trading regime. The central government, however, claims to be aggressively committed to rules prohibiting the employment and requiring the identification and removal of such foreigners, and it has repeatedly tightened the legal and regulatory noose in this regard. But the lack of enforcement of these rules raises serious questions about the government's commitment to them (not unlike in the United States and elsewhere).

In total, all three strategies have served as stopgaps; they have failed to address effectively the economic restructuring and labor market issues that make the case for immigration so compelling or to prepare the country for more immigration. It is the contention of these authors that the need for the latter is becoming increasingly harder to ignore. Although the scale and magnitude of migration into Japan are dwarfed when compared with the experience of virtually any other advanced industrial society (see Table 1), both actual and *feared potential* flows of immigrants have raised concerns in many Japanese quarters that foreigners may soon become a permanent fixture in the Japanese economy and society. As a

---

[4]Consular officers from a variety of advanced industrial societies note that Japanese officials systematically master and then proceed to "game" the immigration systems of their major trading partners. The constant stream of official cable traffic by U.S. consular officials in Japan during the first author's service as a senior U.S. public servant (1988–92) testifies to those officials' frustration with Japan's apparent exploitation of loopholes in the U.S. temporary visa system. Of particular concern has been Japan's successful negotiation of various U.S. entry categories for business visitors, investors (and the essential personnel associated with investment), a variety of temporary workers, and intracompany transferees, among others (classified as B-1, E-1/2, H-1B/H-2B, and L visas, respectively). Conversations of the first author with German, French, and British officials at the time indicated a similar pattern and generated similar expressions of frustration.

TABLE 1.
Foreign or Foreign-Born Population in Selected OECD
Countries, 1997

Country	Thousands*	Percent of Total Population
Japan	1,483	1.2
Spain	610	1.5
Italy	1,241	2.2
United Kingdom	2,066	3.6
Netherlands	678	4.4
Sweden	522	6.0
France	3,597	6.3
Belgium	903	8.9
Germany	7,366	9.0
United States	25,800	9.7
Canada (1996)	4,971	17.4
Switzerland	1,341	19.0
Australia	4,320	23.3

*Numbers for all countries except Australia, Canada, and the United States report the noncitizen population. Figures for Australia, Canada, and the United States represent the entire foreign-born population, including naturalized citizens. Numbers for the European countries do not normally include estimates of the unauthorized population (which is usually 10 to 15 percent of the legal number), nor do they include those among the foreign born who are returning "co-ethnics."

Sources: SOPEMI, *Trends in International Migration*, (Paris: OECD, 1999); Australian Department of Immigration and Multicultural Affairs, *Population Flows: Immigration Aspects* (Canberra: DIMA, January 1999); A. Dianne Schmidley and Campbell Gibson, *Profile of the Foreign-Born Population in the United States: 1997*, U.S. Census Bureau Current Population Report (Washington, D.C.: U.S. Government Printing Office, 1999).

result of these concerns and the relatively high recent levels of unemployment (see Figure 1), Japan finds itself asking where, and particularly how, foreign workers might fit into its long-term economic and social portrait. This question raises issues that begin with Japan's economic competitiveness and end with its cultural identity. It is doubtful that these issues will be resolved without a major reconceptualization of the role of immigration in shaping Japan's future.

It is primarily increased migration from other Asian countries that has brought immigration to the forefront of Japanese policy concerns. As the dominant regional economic superpower,[5] Japan

---

[5]China appears poised to challenge this dominance within the next decade.

FIGURE 1.
Japanese Economic Indicators, 1980–2000

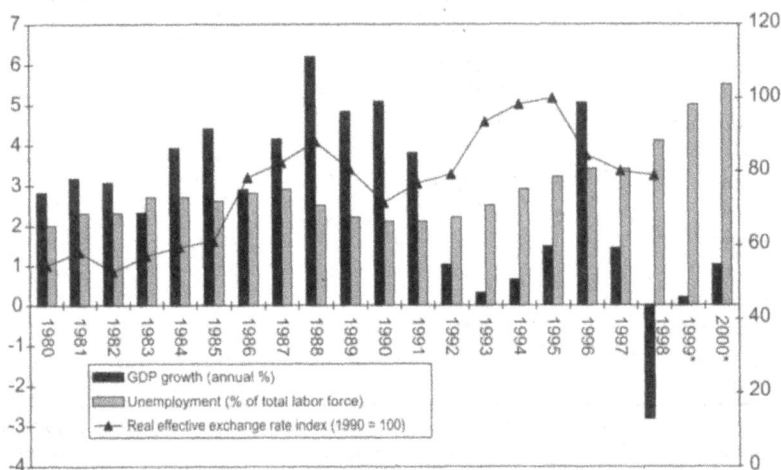

*Projected.
Source: Data from 1980–98 from World Bank, World Development Indicators 2000. Data for 1999–2000 from International Monetary Fund, Japan: Staff Report for the 1999 Article IV Consultation, August 1999.

remains sharply attuned to the regional processes that are transforming the Asian economic horizon. Naturally, how these processes might influence Japan is of primary concern. Unresolved political uncertainties on the Korean peninsula remind Japan that its proximity makes it potentially vulnerable to the consequences of the area's political tensions. These include potential refugee movements—a development that Japan, with its significant Korean minority, could not possibly ignore. The issues surrounding Taiwan's slow and dangerous "dance" with mainland China are also rife with uncertainty. And China, with its vast working-age population, its estimated 200 million unemployed and underemployed, and its vast numbers of internal migrants of rural origin (estimated to exceed 80 million), looms as a potential challenge of the first order for both Japan and the region (Wong 2000; Papademetriou forthcoming). Chinese immigrants, most of whom enter Japan by boat, were estimated to account for 43 percent of illegal entries into Japan in 1997[6] (Japan Immigration Association [JIA] 1998, 87).

In addition, Japan's continuing attractiveness as a destination for immigrants from the broader region cannot be underestimated. The ongoing battle of the Japanese authorities against clandestine immigration testifies to the fact that, despite the economic slump, Japanese jobs and wages (even the most inferior ones) are an enormous magnet to would-be immigrants. Such immigration dovetails in an unlikely manner with the challenges facing Japan as it struggles to maintain its health and social infrastructure at a time when its population is aging quickly. The Organization for Economic Cooperation and Development (OECD) estimates that Japan's pension expenditures will nearly double between 1995 and 2020, compared with a growth rate only one-quarter as large for the United States. Thus, immigration may be the only sure way for Japan to remain both internationally competitive and domestically "solvent," given its precipitously shrinking workforce.[7]

Ironically, Japan—so long a model for those skeptical of the proposition that immigration is an essential ingredient to the growth and prosperity of receiving nations—must prove those skeptics wrong if it is to safeguard its position in the global economy and continue to offer its citizens the services to which they have become accustomed. But welcoming immigrants will not be an easy task. The grappling match between a sort of Japanese exceptionalism—with its deeply embedded sense of social and cultural uniqueness—and the inescapable demographic and economic imperatives will be fascinating to watch. The outcome

---

[6]This figure is based on the number of Chinese among the illegal immigrants apprehended by the government, which Japanese authorities assume is roughly proportionate to the percentage of Chinese among total illegal entries.

[7]Interestingly, the long-term fear of population decline and its potential impact on various parts of society and the economy coexists with short-term population pressures. Part of Japan's reluctance to accept immigrants results from the popular perception that Japan is already bursting at the seams with its own people. Despite significant changes in the structure of the population, Japan still remains a densely populated country, with roughly 336 people per square kilometer on an island not quite as large as California. (By comparison, the United States has roughly 30 people per square kilometer, Germany almost 235, and India 330.) The most important point, however, is that although most Japanese would welcome less crowded conditions, the form that this will take if the status quo continues—lots of old people with progressively fewer young workers whose taxes must pay for needed public services—is simply unviable.

depends on the degree to which Japan is prepared to shed the shrouds of insularity and xenophobia that have defined its relationships with foreigners—and how it chooses to accomplish this. Given its less-than-welcoming historical record, it is unlikely that Japan will grant non-Japanese broad naturalization and citizenship rights during the next decade or so. A more open question is whether, when, and under what circumstances it might grant them full social and labor rights, and even permanent residency rights.

Equally interesting is whether Japan will develop its own immigration path that somehow navigates successfully through what many Japanese policy makers and analysts consider the "mistakes" of other industrialized countries. Foremost among these mistakes is thought to be Europe's failure to manage its "guest worker" programs of the 1960s and 1970s in a manner that could have *prevented* guest workers from turning into permanent residents. This perceived European failure (as well as the social and cultural turmoil in the United States, which many Japanese attribute to U.S. immigration policies) is interpreted by most Japanese opinion leaders as having had adverse social, cultural, and even economic consequences for the receiving societies. Considering the prevalence of these views, the question becomes whether Japan will be able to devise a different way of using immigrant labor—yet one that is consistent with the evolving code of conduct among advanced industrial democracies.

The next decade will reveal the course Japan will follow, giving it the opportunity to demonstrate whether there is indeed another way to manage immigration in a society that finds itself in the grasp of relentless demographic transformation. Barring any unforeseen upswing in the willingness of the Japanese to reproduce themselves,[8] and assuming that Japan wants to offer its elderly the services they need while remaining a global leader, the question of how Japan will choose to conduct its immigration business is likely to be answered sooner rather than later.

---

[8]Even if such an upswing were to occur immediately, the labor market effects would not be felt until sometime in the mid-2020s. In the interim, Japan would be compelled to turn to the immigration choices discussed here.

1. WHY IMMIGRATION NOW MATTERS IN JAPAN

apan became a significant destination for immigrants from a variety of Asian countries as well as from Latin America only in the second half of the 1980s. Japan's history of substantial immigration, however, begins as early as the World War II era,[9] when immigration was used as a way to replace Japanese workers who had been called into military service. Between 1939 and 1945, Japan drew nearly 800,000 workers from the Korean peninsula and 80,000 from China. Indeed, by the end of World War II, Japan was home to more than 2.1 million Koreans, constituting 3.3 percent of the population. Most of these workers left during the postwar period, displaced by returning Japanese military personnel and Japan's economic slowdown. By 1955, only about 550,000 Chinese and Koreans remained (Mori 1997, 34).

Japan, even more than the industrialized European countries, never considered itself a country of immigration. In fact, the presence of the Korean and Chinese workers has been viewed as little more than a residual of Japan's military history. The immigration issue remained largely dormant for years, but in recent decades, a complex mixture of economic, demographic, and political factors has brought immigration closer to the forefront of the Japanese policy debate. The following sections address why immigration has become such an important issue in Japan and why it is likely to remain so in the future.

---

[9] As will be shown later, a significant contingent of Koreans had been in Japan since 1910.

9

THE "HEISEI BOOM" AND THE ONSET OF
LABOR SHORTFALLS

With the end of Japan's lost decade (the 1990s), it is sometimes easy to forget that for most of the 1980s and early 1990s, the Japanese economy experienced a period of extraordinary growth. This period is often referred to as the "Heisei boom" (after the contemporary emperor's reign) or the "bubble economy." The yen's dramatic appreciation in the wake of the 1985 Plaza Accords[10] sparked a seemingly endless process of investment-led economic growth—particularly in the manufacturing and construction sectors—as Japanese business investment between 1984 and 1992 increased by almost 225 percent (Neff 1992, 51). In fact, between 1987 and 1991, Japan registered five of its most robust years of gross domestic product (GDP) growth (see Figure 1). The stronger yen also proved to be an important stimulus for capital investment abroad. With low interest rates, cheap equity capital, impressive productivity gains, cheaper raw material imports, and a series of strategic foreign investment and production relocation decisions, Japan seemed poised to become an even more dominant global economic actor.

Unlike during earlier phases of economic expansion, however, the labor resources necessary to complement the growth in capital investments were not as readily available. During the "Izanagi boom" of the 1960s (named after an ancient deity said to have been present at the birth of the world), for example, Japan was able to rely on its large reservoir of labor in the agricultural, forestry, and fishery sectors. Such options lent the labor market a significant degree of flexibility. Between 1960 and 1973, some 5.2 million workers left agriculture for industrial work—almost half of them doing so between 1965 and 1970 (Mori 1997, 39). The Izanagi boom eventually collapsed during the oil crisis of the mid-1970s, when unemployment between 1973 and 1974 doubled (albeit from a base of only 1.1 percent) and stubbornly stayed at

---

[10]The 1985 Plaza Accords were engineered by then U.S. Treasury Secretary James Baker in an attempt to stem the trade imbalance between Japan and the United States by pushing down the value of the U.S. dollar and thus making U.S. exports "cheaper" in the Japanese market. Between 1985 and the mid-1990s, the value of the yen rose dramatically. From 238 yen to the dollar in 1985, it appreciated over 65 percent to 144 to the dollar in 1990, peaking at less than 90 to the dollar in 1995.

that level for an additional two years. (Unemployment rates of more than 2 percent would not be seen again in Japan until 1992.) By the second half of the 1980s, however, Japan could no longer count on the ready availability of workers from the economy's primary sectors; the total number of remaining rural workers had declined significantly, and so had their willingness to migrate to urban centers. As a result, during the boom years of 1986 to 1991, only 730,000 of the needed workers came from the primary sectors—and only a minority of them came from agriculture (Abella and Mori 1994, 8; Mori 1997, 39).

By the late 1980s, alternative sources of labor were also drying up, including women, who had come to play a key role in the new Japanese economy during the Heisei boom;[11] older workers, who had been rejoining the labor force in measurable ways; and the self-employed. With the traditional reservoirs of workers nearly exhausted, at least within the bounds of what was culturally acceptable and economically feasible, Japan was confronting a serious labor market drought.

The robustness of the Japanese economy had another effect whose broader consequences were mixed. On the one hand, the expanding advancement opportunities for most native workers afforded them great mobility and allowed them to opt for positions that offered the greatest rewards and prestige. This was especially true for younger Japanese, who increasingly viewed blue-collar work as unattractive and distasteful—making *status* in many ways more important than *job security*. On the other hand, upward mobility and the resulting revolution in the expectations of workers, together with the depletion of domestic labor supplies, created ever-larger worker voids in the positions that were less competitive in terms of both status and remuneration. This threatened to undermine Japanese prosperity.

Japanese employers in sectors dominated by "3K" jobs—*kitanai* (dirty), *kitsui* (demanding or difficult), and *kiken* (dangerous)—were the first to feel the pinch. The construction sector, certain segments of low-technology manufacturing, and low

---

[11]The labor force participation rate for women grew by 4 percent in the 1970s and by an additional 3.2 percent during the 1980s (Mori 1997, 40). By 1998, nearly 51 percent of working-age women had entered the labor force (Japan Statistics Bureau 1999a).

value-added service industries across the board were particularly hard hit. In fact, notwithstanding sustained recruiting efforts—which often included offering attractive rewards of "celebration money" and luxury "training getaways"—employment applications in many lower-wage job categories continued to decline, falling by as much as 20 percent in the late 1980s (Hoshiai and Powell 1990, 46). At the same time, the number of job openings continued to climb; by the early 1990s, the proportion of job vacancies to job seekers typically was more than three to two (Japan Statistics Bureau 1996, 96).

Many firms, lacking the financial resources to woo potential employees with signing bonuses or generous benefits, had great difficulty finding applicants willing to spend long hours doing strenuous work for relatively low wages. In fact, by 1992, the construction sector alone was estimated to be nearly 40 percent shy of its full labor complement, a figure that translates into a shortfall of 100,000 workers (Stahl 1992, 30).

THE COLLAPSE OF THE BUBBLE ECONOMY

The early 1990s began to signal economic trouble for Japan. Those same social and economic forces that had helped create the economic juggernaut known as Japan, Inc., were now poised to extract their "pound of flesh" from their creation. Japan's fundamental economic structure came under increasing scrutiny in all its manifestations. This included its banking system and its purchasing and distribution systems (the venerable, if inefficient and controversial, conglomerates known as *keiretsu*) and extended to Japan's extremely well regarded public sector. Most strikingly, Japan's vaunted management system—which only a few years earlier had been held up as a model of quality, innovation, and productivity—came into question.

The results of that scrutiny have been unexpected if not startling, at least for the inattentive. Many of Japan's strengths—Japan's "legacy" to economic competitiveness—have turned out to be grossly unequal to the task of keeping Japan on top of the heap in a world where protective barriers of all sorts have been disappearing. Even lifetime employment,[12] the social glue that traditionally

---

[12]This informal and, until recently, powerful form of social organization was born out of a "social compact" between the business community and the government devel-

cemented employer-employee relations and was one of the pillars on which Japan, Inc., rested, has begun to dry up and weaken. The resulting dramatic rise in suicide rates and the swelling ranks of homeless, unemployed, and new graduates without jobs have made international headlines.[13] Corporate employers can no longer uphold their part of the bargain, and the country has begun to experience an overall weakening of the social contract that had inextricably bound Japanese government, industry, and labor.[14]

The once unthinkable seems to have become reality. Unemployment climbed to and has stood at about 5 percent,[15] levels not seen in more than four decades. The *Financial Times* reported 46 jobs for every 100 job seekers in August 1999 (Abrahams 1999). Overvalued assets and undisciplined lending practices have brought too many of Japan's banks to the brink of insolvency.[16] Corruption within the public sector has tarnished its image and loosened its control over many aspects of Japanese life. Deficits in

---

oped several decades ago. The terms of the compact saw the government offer crucial concessions in areas ranging from taxation and policies that guaranteed high product prices to regulatory and licensing rules that limited competition. In return, employers kept payrolls artificially high (while offering modest pay, benefits, and working conditions) and would refrain from firing workers during economic downturns. This compact is now riddled with holes. According to the *Economist*, about 1 million workers have been "declared redundant" since 1997, and according to one opinion poll, one family in seven has a member who has either lost or expects to lose his or her job (2000a, 26, 27).

[13]An estimated 33,000 suicides in 1999 attributed to layoffs, economic downturns, and forced retirements have left Japan reeling (Struck and Tolbert 2000).

[14]Several large companies have announced cutbacks. For instance, Nissan Motor Company announced in late 1999 its intention to cut nearly 21,000 jobs and close five plants in an attempt to revive the heavily indebted company. The announcement came soon after the purchase of over one-third of the company by French automotive giant Renault. The plan of the French executive who had gained full management control of Nissan was met with extraordinary criticism. Many domestic analysts denounced Nissan's move as irresponsible. According to Akiyama, chairman of the Kansai Economic Federation, "'I doubt the wisdom of destroying your neighbor's house to put out the fire of your own house'" (*Japan Press Weekly* 1999; Harney 1999; Chandler and Tolbert 2000). Even the public sector has not escaped downsizing. The Central Bank has moved to reduce its staff at the behest of the U.S. consulting firm McKinsey. According to some, this is the first time that such moves have been undertaken in the public-sector sphere (Tett 1999).

[15]The *Economist* argues that a more accurate figure is closer to 7 percent, at least when the measurement standards used by other advanced industrial societies are employed (2000a, 26).

[16]Curiously, the Japanese government is now behind 28 percent of direct loans and is heavily involved in indirect lending, believing that the scarcity of private bank lending would actually foster more bankruptcies (*Economist* 1999). Public debt has also soared. For 1999, some estimates place the debt at 120 percent of GDP, more than that of Italy (WuDunn and Kristof 1999).

competitiveness and a protracted recession have forced the reevaluation of Japan's traditional labor market practices and put enormous pressure on the institution of lifetime employment. Bankruptcies of companies have risen; in 1997 bankruptcies numbered 16,365—up by nearly 10,000 since 1990 (Japan Statistics Bureau 1999b, 208).

Small and medium-sized firms have proved particularly vulnerable to Japan's latest round of economic distress. These firms have found themselves in the middle of a "squeeze play" between low productivity and heavy-handed regulation, on the one hand, and aggressive cost-cutting measures by those who traditionally bought their goods and services, on the other hand. This one-two punch has proved lethal for many of them. Faced with stalled domestic demand and a squeeze on lending, many firms in construction, retail, and domestically oriented manufacturing have begun to hurt. And as Japanese global firms look more and more toward lower-cost suppliers in Asia, the United Kingdom, and the United States (*Business Week* 1997)—at least in part because of intense pressure by business groups and worker organizations from countries that have "hosted" extensive Japanese production and distribution facilities—many small and mid-sized domestic suppliers have begun to be sidelined. Making matters worse, Japanese corporations are relying increasingly on *regional* production and employees at a time when *domestic* unemployment has reached a forty-year high (Hirsch and Henry 1997, 13).

The price pinch that Japan's multinationals have been imposing (directly and indirectly) on Japan's small suppliers and subcontractors for more than a decade has further eroded the ability of those suppliers to offer the competitive wages that might have attracted Japanese workers. Such pressure has forced these small firms to tap more directly and systematically into marginal pools of workers in order to survive.[17] Various foreign workers—including Brazilians, Peruvians, and other Latin Americans of Japanese descent (who immigrated to these countries after the United States

---

[17]The fact that native and immigrant workers are employed in discrete labor market segments makes the two groups complementary to each other and effectively limits competition. This phenomenon is fully consistent with an economy's early encounters with labor market–based (or economic) immigration and will be central to Japan's decision about immigration.

14

closed its doors to Japanese immigrants in 1907), but also clandestine workers from China, Korea, and elsewhere in the region—have become a lifeline for many of the small and medium-sized firms that account for nearly two-thirds of Japan's economic output.

Cornelius and Kuwahara (1998) conducted the first comparative field survey on this topic in the San Diego area and in the Japanese manufacturing city of Hamamatsu, and their findings strongly confirm this analysis. Their sample focused on small and newly formed enterprises. As expected, both types of firms were found to be highly dependent on immigrant labor in both cities and, as a result, to have a younger workforce than non–immigrant-dependent firms (18). Not surprisingly, more than half (56 percent) of the highly immigrant-dependent firms in Hamamatsu reported that without foreign workers, they risked either restricting their output severely or closing down altogether (22).

AGING, JAPAN'S WORKFORCE, AND THE JAPANESE FUTURE

Segmenting labor markets have combined with another powerful force—the aging of the population—to complicate Japan's social and economic horizon enormously. Peterson (1999, 43) has called aging the "transcendent economic issue of the 21st century." And while aging is poised to challenge most of the developed world, nowhere is the challenge more imminent or deeper than in Japan. This alone propels the immigration issue onto center stage.

By affecting the size of Japan's workforce, demographic changes hold one of the keys to the long-term viability of Japan's health and retirement security systems, as well as to Japanese economic competitiveness.[18] Since the mid-1950s, Japan's total

---

[18]Of course, demography is not destiny. It is important to acknowledge that demographic projections have sometimes been notoriously wrong. Projections about *labor shortages* are even less reliable, particularly because they fail to accurately anticipate the effects of economic cycles and technological change in creating worker redundancies. For instance, a 1991 projection by the Japanese government estimated that there would be 2.7 million more jobs than workers by the turn of the century (Appleyard and Stahl 1993, 213). An estimate by the Japanese Federation of Economic Organizations predicted a labor shortage of nearly 5 million persons within the same period (Kuptsch and Oishi 1995, 44). What must be kept in mind is that the projections discussed in this text are based primarily on demographic events that have already occurred (births), on trends that are now nearly fifty years old (decreasing fertility), and on trends (such as increasing longevity) about

fertility rate[19] has been falling steadily (Hoshiai and Powell 1990, 47) and has fallen by more than 25 percent since 1970.[20] It now stands at an estimated 1.4 percent, among the world's lowest rates (see Figure 2).[21] The forces driving this decrease in fertility include

FIGURE 2.
Japanese Total Fertility Rates (per woman), 1950–2000

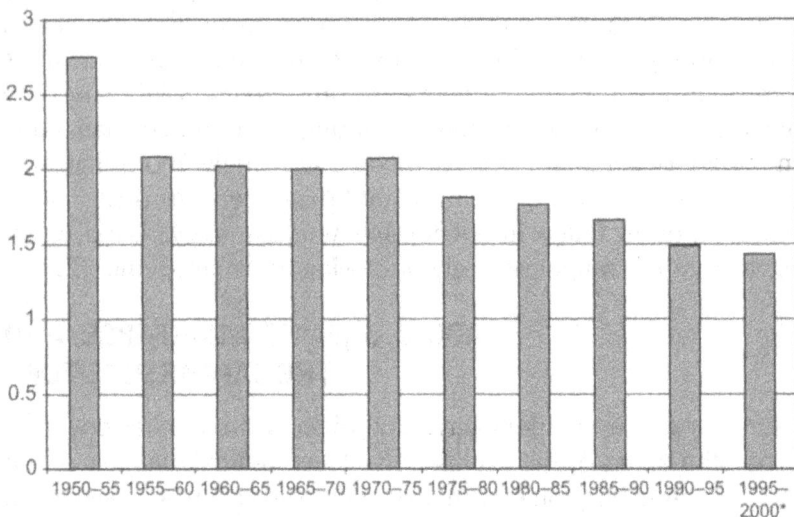

*Projected.
Source: Population Division, Department of Economic and Social Affairs of the United Nations Secretariat, *World Population Prospects: The 1998 Revision* (New York: UN, 1999).

which there is little disagreement. The issue, then, is not how many jobs may or may not be needed but how standards of living can be maintained and who is going to pay for maintaining them.

[19]*Total fertility rate* (TFR) measures the average number of children that would be born per female if all females lived to the end of their childbearing years and bore children according to a given fertility rate at each age (United Nations Population Division 1997).

[20]In 1997, the Japanese total fertility rate dropped to a postwar low of 1.39. This is not as low as in some European countries, such as Italy, Germany, and Spain, where birthrates are even lower.

[21]Some Japanese companies have taken unusual steps to encourage employees to have larger families. One toy maker offers employees 1 million yen (a little less than $10,000) for every baby they have after their second child. The public sector is also trying to play a role in reversing declines in fertility by focusing on the costs of raising children (offering modest monetary subsidies) and by encouraging more "family-friendly" work environments (Sims 2000a). One must be skeptical, however, about the ability of such measures to reverse patterns that are now embedded in household dynamics and, more importantly, in the broader social culture.

improved birth control technologies, increased affluence,[22] and higher female participation in the labor force.

This decades-long, below-replacement-level fertility rate, together with inexorable increases in longevity, means that the Japanese population has been aging at unprecedented rates. In fact, in 1997, the size of the cohort of those who were sixty-five years of age or older *surpassed* the size of the one- to fifteen-year-old cohort. The UN Population Division estimates that the size of the former cohort will grow rapidly over the next two decades, accounting for more than one-quarter of Japan's total population before its growth begins to slow (see Figure 3).

In the next two decades, as Japan's baby boom generation passes from economic activity to retirement, even higher old-age

FIGURE 3.
Population Projections for Japan (in millions), 1995–2050

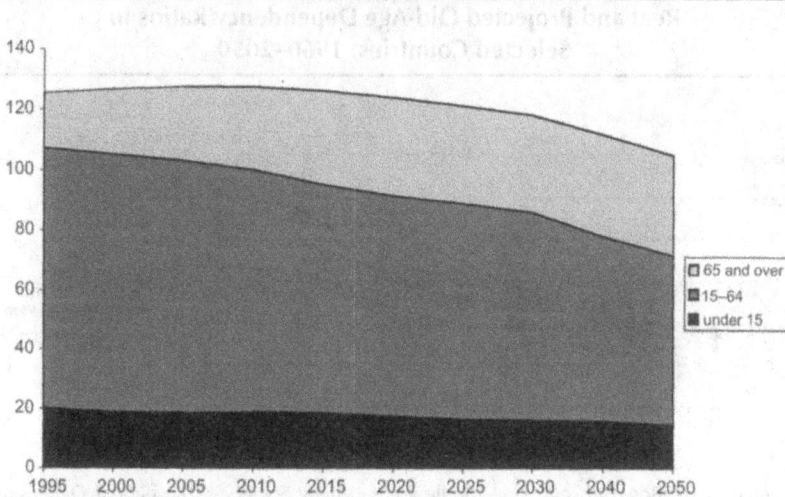

Source: Population Division, Department of Economic and Social Affairs of the United Nations Secretariat, *World Population Prospects: The 1998 Revision* (New York: UN, 1999).

---

[22]Affluence in most instances is closely tied to the earning of two professional incomes. With it go not only a much greater need for personal services of all types (which in turn makes the two incomes necessary) but also a commitment to a career, with its associated demands. Nothing in this scenario suggests any possibility of higher fertility rates. Adding the costs of raising and educating children to the mix makes the prospects for increased fertility even less realistic.

dependency ratios[23] will follow. The evidence is compelling. As Figure 4 shows, the estimated dependency ratios of Japan (along with those of Germany) will deteriorate dramatically in the next twenty years, while those for the United States, the United Kingdom, and France will increase neither as quickly nor as deeply. Table 2 makes a similar point. By the year 2020, only the United States, Canada, Australia, and Luxembourg are projected to have dependency ratios below 30 percent.[24] Notably, all four are also states of high immigration. Japan's ratio will stand at 42 percent. This means that, on average, the income (and taxes) of fewer than two and a half Japanese workers will be expected to support each Japanese who is not in the labor market.

The challenges of this scenario are significant. Securing adequate living standards for pensioners without putting unprecedented tax burdens on workers will become more difficult every

FIGURE 4.
Real and Projected Old-Age Dependency Ratios in Selected Countries, 1960–2050

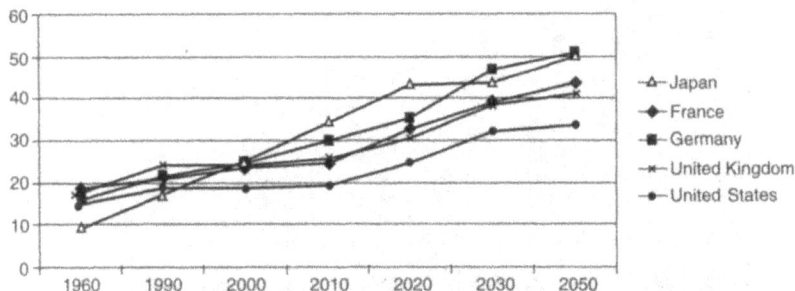

Source: Barry Bosworth and Gary Burtless eds., *Aging Societies: The Global Dimension* (Washington, D.C.: Brookings Institution Press, 1998), p. 3. Primary sources: National sources. Data for France are from Eduard Bos et al., *World Population Projections, 1994–95* ed. (Baltimore: World Bank and Johns Hopkins University Press, 1994).

[23]The old-age dependency ratio is the ratio of people aged sixty-five and over to those aged fifteen to sixty-four.

[24]It is important to note again that for the period under discussion, the values of most of the variables are certain.

TABLE 2
Projected Old-Age Dependency Ratios for 2010 and 2020
in Selected OECD Countries

Country	Ratio of Those Aged 65 and over to Those Aged 15 to 64* (percent)		Additional Working-Age Population Required in 2020 for Old-Age Dependency Ratio to Remain at 2010 Levels (thousands)	Estimates of Net Migration for Period 1985 to 1995† (thousands)
	2010	2020		
Australia	19.0	24.6	4,380	930
Belgium	25.1	31.3	1,620	150
Canada	20.4	28.0	8,600	1,490
France	25.6	33.0	10,950	630
Germany	27.7	30.0	4,700	4,560
Greece	29.6	33.6	900	420
Italy	30.4	36.4	6,760	850
Japan	32.3	42.0	22,350	−140
Luxembourg	23.0	27.9	60	30
Netherlands	22.4	31.0	4,040	340
Spain	26.2	30.6	4,280	−80
Sweden	27.9	34.2	1,290	280
Switzerland	24.6	31.7	1,430	370
United Kingdom	25.0	30.1	7,640	720
United States	19.2	25.4	66,410	5,800

*Old-age dependency ratios calculated from medium variant projections in United Nations, Department of Economic and Social Affairs, Population Division, *World Population Prospects: The 1996 Revision*, (New York: UN, 1998).
†Estimates of net migration calculated as residual of population change and natural increase published in *Labour Force Statistics* (Paris: OECD, 1997).

Source: SOPEMI, *Trends in International Migration* (Paris: OECD, 1998), p.

decade. The sums involved are immense. The OEC
estimated that the unfunded pension liabilities in the
world stand at about $34 trillion. In fact, baseline pens
ditures as a percentage of GDP for the five countries rep
Figure 4 would increase substantially—and in Japan's
metrically—between the years 2000 and 2020. For in
France, they would increase from 9.8 to 11.6; for Gerr
11.5 to 12.3; for the United Kingdom, from 4.5 to 5.1;
United States, from 4.2 to 5.2. The increase for Japan
would be the greatest by far: from 7.5 percent of G[
percent.

Similarly, paying for medical care for the elderly adds another $30 trillion to the developed world's present liabilities. This figure will continue to grow apace with the size of the aged cohort—especially when considering that those over sixty-five years of age consume between two and four times as much in medical benefits as the rest of the population and that the rates for those over seventy-five are much higher.

Finally, severe and persistent labor shortages, as well as mismatches between needed and available skills, will redefine the world of work in most advanced societies.

Japan and the rest of the developed world have some ammunition with which to combat some of these challenges. They could mandate longer work lives, reduce publicly supported benefits (both retirement and health benefits), create new or additional privately funded retirement systems, and engage in a new and more severe round of fundamental economic restructuring.[25] However, in the long run, most efforts to prolong the status quo and defer the more comprehensive set of interventions implied by this analysis are likely to prove insufficient. Ultimately, Japan will have to rely more heavily on foreigners for an increasing number of important social and economic purposes. Among them are tending to the needs of its affluent but aged population, keeping retirement and public health systems afloat, and, in many cases, keeping production systems humming.[26]

The data in Table 2 make this startlingly clear. In view of the duration and depth of Japan's low fertility rate, if it is to maintain dependency ratios in 2020 that stay at 2010 levels, it will require labor force increases (native workers who enter the labor market for the first time, workers who postpone or return from retirement

---

[25]Japan has already begun to take steps along these lines. For example, on March 28, 2000, the Japanese parliament voted to cut pension benefits for new retirees by 5 percent and raise the retirement age gradually from sixty to sixty-five (Kashiwagi and Chandler 2000).

[26]The Japanese are aware of this reality. Several recent government reports have emphasized the need to open up to foreigners as a way of dealing with the aging population. The Ministry of Justice recently recommended that thought be given to admitting foreign health care workers. However, several government ministries, including the Health and Welfare Ministry, strongly objected to this suggestion, arguing that doing so would contradict Japan's policy of not admitting unskilled foreign workers (Toriyama 2000). On the local level, at least one program to recruit foreigners to work as home health care aides for the elderly already exists (Tolbert 2000b).

and are flexible enough to "reskill" themselves, plus foreign workers) that are much larger than the size of each cohort for the 1985–95 period.[27] A recent United Nations study suggests even more strongly that Japan will need much more immigration in the future. Based on certain assumptions,[28] the study estimates that from 1995 to 2050, Japan will need 17 million immigrants (an average of 343,000 net additions annually) if it is to prevent its population from declining. Likewise, to prevent a decline in the size of its working-age population (ages fifteen to sixty-four) during the same period, Japan will need nearly 33.5 million immigrants (an average of 647,000 annually). (United Nations Population Division 2000, 2). Even with corresponding changes in the other variables that affect the size of a workforce most directly—such as changing the retirement age[29] and making a true effort to bring women, retirees, or the disabled *fully* into the labor force—Japanese reliance on immigrants will likely increase strongly by the new century's second decade.

EXTERNAL INFLUENCES ON IMMIGRATION TO JAPAN

As we have argued, Japan will become a more central player in the global migration system in the years ahead. The forces that will impel it deeper into that system will be both domestic (the focus of the discussion until now) and external, particularly regional. Externally, the area to watch is Japan's immediate region. Migration within East and Southeast Asia is likely to grow significantly in the next fifteen years as the region's economic dynamism resumes, the

---

[27]Projections about the number of natives likely to enter the labor market and about those sixty-five years old or older are very reliable for the next two decades. Even if fertility were to increase dramatically in the near future, it would have no practical effect on the dependency ratios until more than twenty years after the increase (when the newborn population graduates from university or completes technical training).

[28]The study's estimates are based on the medium variant population projections of the UN's *World Population Prospects: 1998 Revision*. The study's calculations assume 1995 fertility levels and zero net migration after 1995. To allow cross-country comparisons, the study assumes that migration to Japan (and all other countries in the study) has the average age and sex structure of migration into the United States, Canada, and Australia and that immigrants experience the average fertility and mortality conditions of their country of destination after they arrive (United Nations Population Division 2000, 13–15). Different assumptions would affect the estimates accordingly.

[29]The same UN study estimates that Japan would have to mandate a retirement age of seventy-seven years in order to achieve the same dependency ratio in 2050 as it had in 1995 (United Nations Population Division 2000, 50).

labor forces of some key countries (such as Korea and Taiwan) age, and migration flows—and the institutions and private networks that support them—become more mature.

The continent of Asia has had the world's largest intraregional migration flows for most of the last thirty-five years, ranging from about 42 percent of the total in the mid-1960s to about 36 percent in 1990 (Papademetriou forthcoming). For much of that time, the oil-producing countries of western Asia and, since the 1980s, the rapidly growing countries of East and Southeast Asia (concentrated in three geographical nodes: Japan, Singapore-Malaysia, and Hong Kong–Taiwan–Korea) have been the strongest poles of attraction (Massey et al. 1998).

Despite Japan's recent economic crisis, Asian migration into Japan has continued. Asia accounted for more than 50 percent of legal foreign entries into Japan in 1998 (see Figure 5). The enormous labor surpluses in lesser-developed countries in the region, such as China, the Philippines, Thailand, Bangladesh, Pakistan, and, until recently, Malaysia and Korea, have created a persistent economic "push" from without. Most of these countries have much younger populations than Japan's and, hence, high rates of labor force growth. They offer, however, grossly inadequate opportunities for domestic employment. In addition, the enormous wage differentials between most of these countries and Japan make even the most poorly compensated work in Japan more desirable than skilled and professional work at home (Conference on International Manpower Flows 1991). Furthermore, with the decline of oil prices in the 1980s, migrants who once sought employment in the Middle East are now turning toward Japan (Kashiwazaki 1998, 239).

In the coming years, Asia's intraregional migration can be expected to rise despite the absence of a formal tradition of immigration in most countries in the region. Four forces will be responsible for this development:

- Labor supply shortfalls for several of the rapidly developing countries in the region—with Japan being the primary example—as a result of low fertility and aging populations.
- The by now strong and increasing tradition of emigration by the nationals of most countries in the region.
- Unresolved political conflicts (such as on the Korean peninsula and between China and Taiwan).

FIGURE 5.
Legal Foreign Entries into Japan, 1998

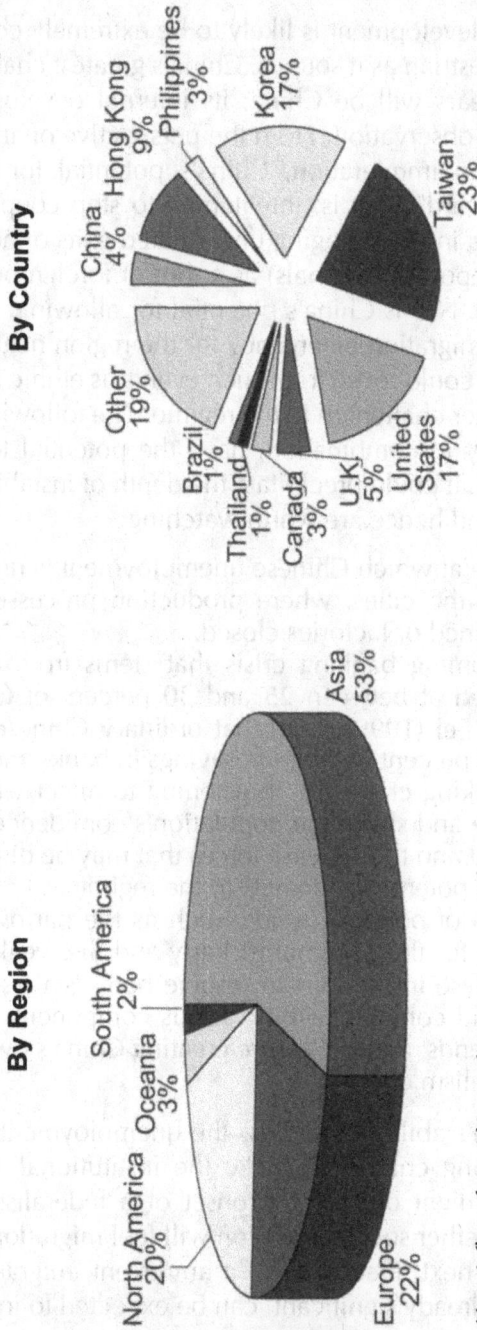

By Country

Korea 17%

Taiwan 23%

Philippines 3%

Hong Kong 9%

China 4%

Other 19%

Brazil 1%

Thailand 1%

Canada 3%

U.K. 5%

United States 17%

Note: Due to rounding, percents do not total 100.

By Region

Asia 53%

Europe 22%

North America 20%

Oceania 3%

South America 2%

Note: Inflows from Africa and nonstates account for less than 1 percent of total inflows.

Note: Excludes reentries.

Source: Japanese Ministry of Justice, Annual Report of Statistics on Legal Migrants, 1999.

- The likely reemergence of political instability in China—with its potential as a destabilizing agent for the entire region.

The last development is likely to be extremely consequential for Japan. Pedestrian as it sounds, China's greatest challenge in the next fifteen years will be China; its internal developments thus demand close observation. From the perspective of an assessment that focuses on immigration, China's potential for playing the "immigration card" (that is, threatening to stop cooperating with other countries in discouraging unregulated exits or accepting the return of its deported nationals) as a tool of foreign policy cannot be overlooked. Nor is China's potential for allowing, or even creating, a mass migration emergency for the region negligible. Such an emergency could result from such events as ethnic tensions that go awry or other challenges to the regime. The following three factors, especially in combination, have the potential to create the type of crisis that could precipitate the depth of instability contemplated here, and hence are worth watching:

- The rate at which Chinese unemployment is rising, particularly in the cities, where production processes are being streamlined or factories closed.
- The looming banking crisis that stems from bad loans—estimated at between 25 and 30 percent of China's GDP. Minxin Pei (1999) notes that ordinary Chinese have more than 80 percent of their life savings in banks and argues that the banking crisis—by threatening to affect virtually every Chinese and shake the population's confidence in the government and thus release forces that may be difficult to contain—is potentially "lethal" to the regime.
- A series of political trends, such as the narrowing base of support for the Communist Party and the weakened ability of Chinese institutions to resolve both "state-society" conflicts and conflicts within various components of the state. Such trends, argues Pei, are creating China's own version of a federalism crisis.

Clearly, China's ability to address the unemployment crisis, manage the banking crisis, and make the institutional and political reforms that might obviate the onset of a federalism crisis will determine whether social explosion will fuel migration emergency threats in the next fifteen years. In any event, migration pressure from China, already significant, can be expected to increase.

2. A PROFILE OF JAPAN'S FOREIGN POPULATION

Nearly 1.8 million foreigners live in Japan (see Table 3). A third of these are special permanent residents,[30] mostly Koreans granted special status under the 1952 Treaty of Peace. Regular permanent residents and their family members are relatively few, accounting for less than 6 percent of the total foreign population. Japanese immigration policy does not have a permanent immigrant category for newcomers. However, regular permanent residency can be obtained after a significant stay in Japan. The only explicit criteria for permanent residency are the following: the applicant must be of "good conduct" and have sufficient assets to live independently, and the applicant's permanent residency must "coincide with the interests of Japan." Other than these criteria, the process of granting permanent residency is extremely opaque (for example, there is no set number of years of residency required to achieve permanent status) (Johnstone 1996).

Although Japan does not allow foreigners to enter the country under permanent immigrant status, certain groups can enter as "long-term residents" without restrictions on their employment; spouses and children of Japanese nationals, foreigners with children born of Japanese nationals (for example, the non-Japanese parent of a child born out of wedlock with a Japanese national), and *Nikkeijin* all fall under this category (see Table 3 for statistics).

All other legal immigrants must enter under a temporary status—either as skilled immigrants under specific employment

---

[30]Since 1992, the Japanese government has classified the population of ethnic Koreans and Taiwanese remaining in Japan after World War II as "special permanent residents" (Johnstone 1996).

TABLE 3.
Foreign Population by Country of Origin and Status of Stay in Japan as of January 1, 1999

Country of Origin	Special Permanent Residents	Registered (Documented)										Without Documents	Total
		Professional, Technical and Skilled Workers	Cultural, Religious, and Other Activities	Entertainment, Show Business	On the job Training	Studies	Visits with Relatives	Short Stay	Long-term Stay	Permanent Residents and Their Families	Others	Visa Overstays	
Koreas	528,450	7,463	441	695	240	18,604	11,435	6,499	31,494	30,615	971	62,577	699,484
China	4,349	31,620	10,543	931	15,646	52,420	30,408	6,974	84,840	32,646	398	44,237	315,012
Brazil	14	250	42	199	217	406	297	1,895	214,359	2,691	193	—	220,563
Philippines	21	1,463	1,687	24,278	2,122	1,129	724	4,972	54,004	10,907	2,479	40,420	144,206
Thailand	1	807	170	103	1,865	1,622	252	4,584	10,762	948	1,860	30,065	53,039
Peru	2	59	10	5	52	74	55	6,651	30,475	3,285	122	10,320	51,110
U.S.	181	16,951	483	223	15	1,285	6,557	746	11,483	4,677	55	—	42,656
Malaysia	4	544	18	46	314	2,254	413	1,609	1,017	349	20	9,989	16,577
Indonesia	3	300	4,968	285	3,709	1,395	1,039	748	2,117	297	70	—	14,931
Iran	5	152	18	3	11	156	318	4,802	1,103	227	349	7,304	14,448
Bangladesh	1	511	59	2	88	1,296	1,035	2,452	581	101	237	4,936	11,299
Pakistan	6	363	26	19	42	164	389	2,700	1,347	282	554	4,307	10,199
Myanmar	1	380	34	5	67	951	230	2,356	358	58	59	5,487	9,986
Others	358	29,296	4,891	2,077	2,720	8,583	12,523	12,827	32,179	12,500	1,031	51,406	170,391
Total	533,396	90,159	23,390	28,871	27,108	90,339	65,675	59,815	476,119	99,583	8,398	271,048	1,773,901

Source: Ministry of Justice, Zairyu Gaikokujin Tokei, 1998 [Statistics on Registered Foreigners, 1998] (Tokyo: Ministry of Justice, 1999).

categories or as trainees under a special program that allows unskilled workers to enter Japan for job training. Other than spouses and children of Japanese nationals, *Nikkeijin*, and trainees—who may be unskilled—unskilled workers are not permitted legal entry into Japan. In numerical terms, economically active foreigners, not including permanent residents, account for over a quarter of the legal foreign population (calculation based on data from Japan Ministry of Justice 1999; SOPEMI 1999a).[31] About a third of these workers are registered under a specific employment category. Among these categories, "specialist in humanities and international services" (26 percent), "entertainer" (24 percent), and "engineer" (13 percent) contain the most legal registrants. Persons of Japanese descent and the spouses and children of Japanese nationals or of permanent residents account for over half the legal foreign workers in Japan. In terms of the composition of the legal foreign population, Koreans are the most numerous, followed by Chinese and Brazilians (see Table 3 and Figure 6).

According to government figures, approximately 15 percent of the foreign population in Japan is unauthorized (Japan Ministry of Justice 1999), numbering 251,697 as of January 1, 2000.[32] This number represents a decline from a peak of almost 300,000 unauthorized immigrants in 1993 (*Kyodo News* 2000). Stepped-up enforcement efforts and the economic crisis have been among the factors contributing to this decline.

Over the last twenty years, the demographic profile and occupational structure of the unauthorized population have changed significantly. In the early and mid-1980s, clandestine foreign workers in Japan were typically young, female, and from the Philippines, Taiwan, or Thailand. Of the unauthorized workers apprehended in 1984, for instance, 93 percent were women, and 62 percent were Filipino (Spencer 1992, 756). Most were recruited to work in Japan's entertainment industry and served primarily as bar hostesses, sex workers, or dancers. Filipina entertainers, who

---

[31]Nonworking students, nonworking spouses and children of Japanese nationals or of permanent residents, and persons visiting relatives and family are among the groups that make up the other 75 percent of the foreign population that is not registered as working.

[32]Since 1990, the Japanese Immigration Bureau within the Ministry of Justice has tracked visa overstayers as a proxy for unauthorized immigrants in search of employment. These figures should be viewed as low-end ones because they do not include unauthorized immigrants who *entered* the country illegally.

FIGURE 6.
Foreign Population by Nationality, 1998

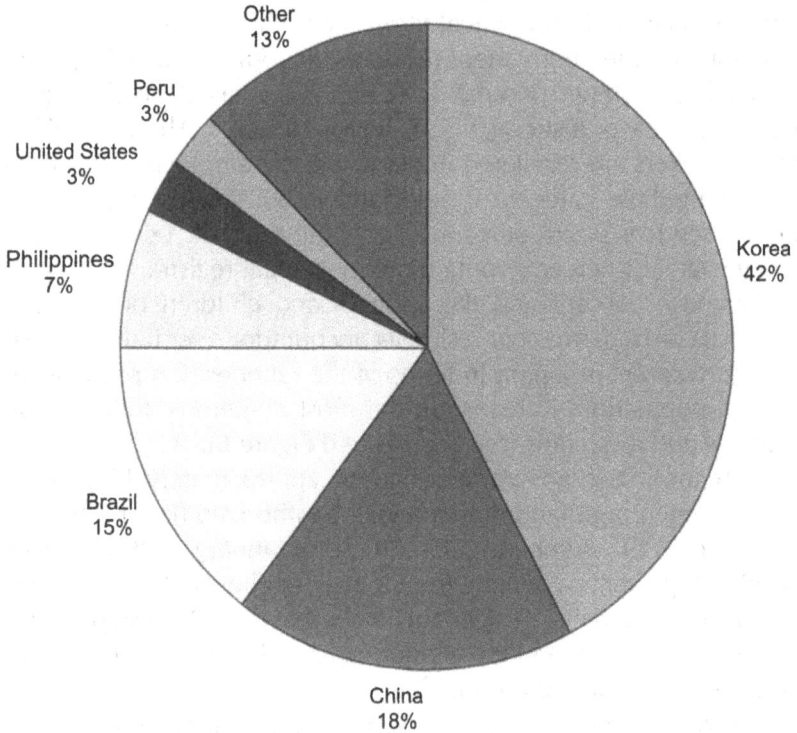

Note: Figures represent the number of registered foreigners. Foreigners in Japan must register after ninety days of residence. Due to rounding, percents do not total 100.
Source: Japanese Immigration Bureau, Ministry of Justice, Statistics on Foreign Residents; see Japan Information Network at http://jin.jcic.or.jp.

made up the majority of unauthorized entertainers, began coming to Japan in large numbers when public pressure curtailed Japanese sex tours to the Philippines, which had been numerous in the 1970s (Piquero-Ballescas 1998, 84).

With the Heisei boom, however, the unauthorized population began to change. The segmentation of the labor market that began during this period created opportunities in low-wage sectors. As the demand for semiskilled and unskilled labor increased (without a concomitant loosening of the immigration policy), the number of backdoor (unauthorized) immigrants rose, and they became increasingly concentrated in low-skilled positions. Soon, the typical clandestine foreigner could be found working in the construction and manufacturing sectors. In fact, by the early 1990s, these two sectors of the Japanese labor market accounted for nearly 50 percent of unauthorized foreign workers (JIA 1995, 43). A growing number had also begun to obtain jobs in such low-wage, low-value-added service jobs as dishwashing, deliveries, waiting tables, janitorial services, and retailing (Spencer 1992, 757; JIA 1995, 44).

Today, most unauthorized workers are young, single Asian men, particularly from Korea, China, the Philippines, Thailand, Iran, and Malaysia—countries that accounted for 78 percent of the official estimate of the total unauthorized working population in 1997 (JIA 1998, 87, 89) (see Figure 7). Women make up nearly 40 percent of the total (JIA 1998, 89), and although over half are still employed as hostesses or waitresses, some are beginning to move into the industrial and commercial sectors. In 1997, 14 percent of the unauthorized female workers who were apprehended worked in factories (JIA 1998, 96).

Visa overstays account for the vast majority of immigration offenses recorded by the government[33] (see Figure 8). Seventy-five percent of unauthorized immigrants apprehended by the government enter the country on tourist visas. Others, particularly Chinese and Koreans, arrive as students (4.5 percent) and violate the terms of their visas (*Kyodo News* 2000).[34] Another 5 percent of unauthorized immigrants enter as entertainers. Among women, especially, entertainment visas continue to be a vehicle for unauthorized immigration: of those women who overstayed their visas in 1997, nearly 8 percent entered as entertainers (JIA 1998, 90).[35] And although they have since been suspended, Japan's bilateral

---

[33]In 1998, 82 percent of apprehensions were overstays (JIA 1999, 74).

[34]In 1997, over 90 percent of clandestine workers who entered as students were either Chinese or Korean (JIA 1998, 91–92).

[35]Representatives of Japanese *yakuza*, or organized crime syndicates, are thought to recruit many of these female migrants under false pretenses. Lured into Japan with promises of legitimate employment in the entertainment, sales, and manufacturing industries, they are informed upon arrival that they have incurred debts as high as ¥4 million (US$40,000) in the form of travel expenses and other "fees" and that they must repay these debts through prostitution. To prevent their escape, the women are typically stripped of their passports, threatened with violence, and monitored constantly. For an indefinite period, they are sold or traded through a clandestine network of bars and brothels. Seeking outside assistance is extremely difficult for these women. Even when escape is possible,

FIGURE 7.
Unauthorized Foreign Workers by Country, 1997

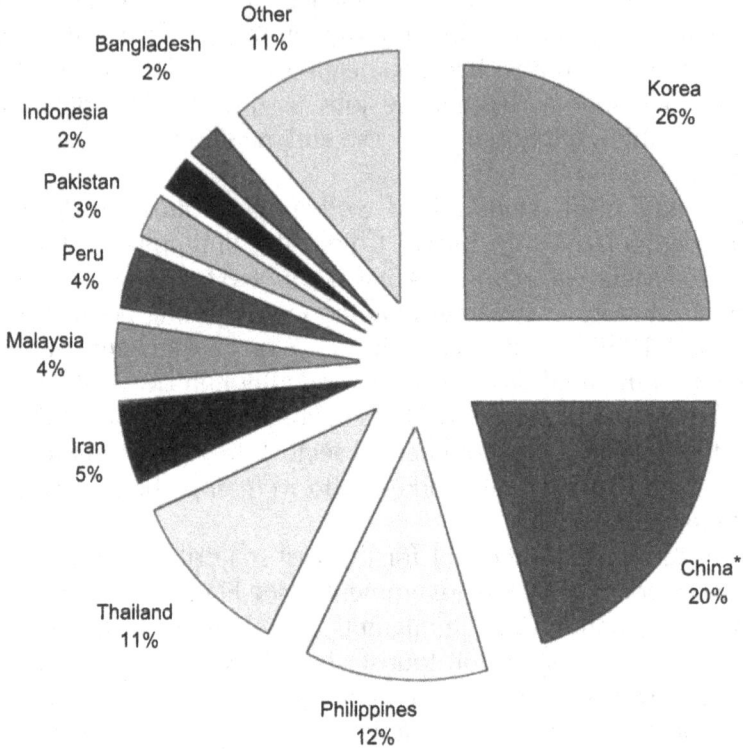

Note: Numbers represent workers against whom deportation procedures were initiated. Due to rounding, percents do not total 100.
*Includes Taiwan and Hong Kong.
Source: Japan Immigration Association, *1997 Statistics on Immigration Control* (Tokyo: JIA, 1998).

the majority of them are unable to communicate or otherwise navigate their surroundings. Those caught up in the nationwide sex industry are further isolated because most Japanese are either indifferent or antagonistic to them. (In fact, xenophobes in Japan have characterized AIDS as a foreigner's disease, and Thai prostitutes, in particular, are charged with having introduced the virus to an otherwise "pure" Japanese society.) Were it not for publicized accounts of women who have murdered their captors, the plight of these migrants would still be ignored. As a result of such publicity, however, several prominent Japanese women, including journalists and politicians, have begun organizing and speaking out on behalf of women forced into prostitution. Additionally, countries such as the Philippines have tightened restrictions on the overseas hiring of their female nationals (Oka 1994, 57).

arrangements with Bangladesh, Iran, and Pakistan were meant to foster commerce and trade by allowing reciprocal visa-free entry. Instead, these agreements provided an opportunity for many nationals of these countries to take advantage of the visa exemptions to enter and work illegally in Japan (Hormats et al. 1993).

FIGURE 8.
Number of Violations of the Immigration Control Act by Category, 1990–98

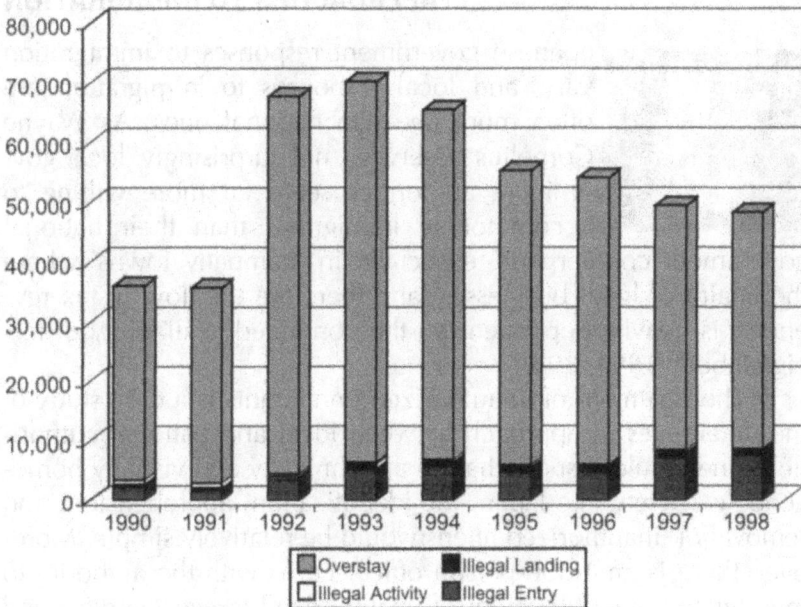

Source: Japan Immigration Association, *1994* and *1998 Statistics on Immigration Control* (Tokyo: JIA, 1995, 1999).

3. JAPANESE RESPONSES TO IMMIGRATION

TURNING A BLIND EYE: LOCAL VERSUS NATIONAL APPROACHES TO IMMIGRATION

apanese government responses to immigration vary, and local responses to immigration are often more lax than national ones. As Wayne Cornelius observes, "not surprisingly, local government authorities seem far more willing to accommodate immigrants than their national government counterparts, especially in 'company towns' where the health of local businesses (and therefore the flow of tax revenues) is heavily dependent on the continued availability of foreign labor" (1994, 394).

The treatment of unauthorized immigrants is a case study of the differences in approach between local and national authorities. One would assume that, in an ethnically and visually homogeneous society like Japan, the identification, apprehension, and removal of unauthorized aliens would be relatively simple. Moreover, there is an 1,800-person officer corps with the authority to investigate the employment of unauthorized foreign workers and an even larger number of local officials to help it enforce what in the United States are known as "employer sanctions" (Cornelius 1994, 392). This is more than twice the compliance officer corps of the U.S. Department of Labor's Wage and Hour Division (which is responsible for enforcing most U.S. labor laws) and about five times larger than the comparable group at the U.S. Immigration and Naturalization Service.

Stacked against these investigative resources are two factors. First is the reality that clandestine workers in Japan, as elsewhere, maintain relatively low visibility, and their employment in Japan's myriad smaller firms, usually in positions that keep them away from the public eye, makes the enforcement of applicable laws difficult. Second is the equally reasonable fact that local authorities are deeply ambivalent about clandestine foreign workers because of their willingness to do the kinds of jobs that few Japanese are interested in doing. In this scenario, the growth of Japan's unauthorized immigration problem may have less to do with having the ability or resources to find these foreign workers and more with there being an understandable reluctance to ferret them out (Cornelius and Kuwahara 1998, 3).

The speculation that local officials may in fact view most foreign workers not as a threat to the Japanese economy but as a necessary complement to it—and act accordingly—finds further support in the case of the on-again, off-again debate over civil service employment for foreigners. Many local governments have partially or fully eliminated nationality requirements for civil service positions, often against the wishes of the central government.[36] In 1996, for example, the Tokyo suburb of Kawasaki voted to abolish the nationality requirement for municipal public servants, making it the first major city in Japan to open its jobs to non-Japanese (*Mainichi Daily News* 1996a). In a vivid illustration of the local-national tension on the issue of foreign workers, the Kawasaki move was immediately attacked by national leaders. Home Affairs Minister Hiroyuki Kurata announced that the "position taken by the Home Affairs Ministry [is] that people who exercise administrative authority must be Japanese nationals. It [the nationality requirement] is an undoubted principle of law for public servants, . . . it is not an issue that can be discussed together with local autonomy." The announcement concluded on a conciliatory note, with the minister committing to "continue to seek an understanding by the city of Kawasaki"(Japan Economic News-wire 1996, 5). The Kawasaki mayor's reply pointed out that "the government has no clear-cut judgments or criteria with regard to the exercise of power or the formation of the will of the state"[37] (*Mainichi Daily News* 1996b).

---

[36]A 1993 government survey found that 354 of the 1,195 local governments responding had eliminated nationality requirements for civil service positions (Johnstone 1996).

[37]In a concession to national authorities, Kawasaki passed a second ordinance to reserve section chief and higher-level positions, as well as positions in the fire department, for Japanese nationals.

Local responses to immigration are linked to the larger Japanese debate about the devolution of authority to local government. Decentralization has been a hot topic in Japan in recent years. On April 1, 2000, the Bill to Adjust Related Laws in Order to Promote Decentralization took effect. Under the bill, prefecture governors and local mayors are no longer considered officials of the central government, and local government duties are classified as either "autonomous" or "legally delegated" national government tasks. The new law also dictates that central government involvement must have a foundation in law, be kept to the minimum required to meet objectives, take into account the autonomy of local authorities, and be carried out in a fair and transparent manner (Japan Local Government Center [JLGC] 1999). This legislation promises to augment the trend toward local involvement in immigration issues described earlier.

Of course, "ambivalence" is a difficult variable to measure, and in Japan, as elsewhere, it has varied in intensity with economic and other factors. There is, however, an increasingly striking contrast between Japan's official adoption of anti-immigrant positions, which deny most—but particularly clandestine—foreigners benefits and rights, and the seemingly more complacent attitude of local officials, who in many cases turn a blind eye to the foreigners on whom small to medium-sized firms rely. In addition to its challenge to policy and governance, this dynamic is part of the process that extends to foreign workers and their employers an economic lifeline yet fosters their exploitation.

THE RIGHTS OF FOREIGN WORKERS AND THE 1990 IMMIGRATION CONTROL ACT

Adaptation to Japanese society is a challenge to most foreigners, regardless of legal status. Most foreign workers live and work in Japan's metropolitan centers, particularly in Tokyo and Osaka, although some also find employment in agriculture (Sassen 1998, 65). In 1994, Tokyo alone was estimated to be home to nearly 20 percent of the nation's foreign workers and over 30 percent of its clandestine ones (JIA 1995, 42, 58). Clandestine workers are typically able to secure employment in small and medium-sized factories that subcontract for larger Japanese firms by relying on rather efficient ethnic networks that underwrite the cost of travel and connect them with prospective employers. The managers of these factories report that they have no recourse but to solicit foreigners willing to risk working without proper documentation (Asahi News Service 1992). Because unskilled and semiskilled work has been abundant in Japan, foreign workers have tended to ignore, or at least to endure, the often difficult conditions that go along with living as a foreigner in Japan.

Given the high urban concentration in Japan, finding adequate housing is one of the first challenges that foreign workers must overcome. The challenge is much greater for clandestine foreigners; most are without guarantors or character references, and many Japanese landlords refuse to accept them as tenants (Jones 1992; Oka 1994). Discrimination and high rents force many foreigners to find shelter in overcrowded apartments or even in the nation's public parks.[38] Furthermore, for those whose presence in Japan is unauthorized, neither they nor their families have a right to health insurance or most types of social services. If there are children involved, they are denied government services, including education and health care (Silverman 1992). When in need of medical care, they are turned away by hospitals that refuse to accept uninsured patients.[39]

Despite acknowledging their dependence on foreign labor, the behavior of many Japanese employers seems to compound the hardships experienced by clandestine immigrants. Foreign workers complain of unscrupulous employers that violate basic labor protections[40] and even their human rights with impunity, because unauthorized migrants do not enjoy the full protection of the law (Kurtenbach 1992). Many are denied the benefits that are regularly accorded to native and other legal workers, including paid holidays and overtime (set at a minimum of 25 percent above the regular hourly wage). This latter benefit is particularly significant,

---

[38]Tokyo's Ueno Park, for example, was infamous for the many Iranians who made their home there in the early 1990s (Jones 1992).

[39]Tadashi Hanami (1998, 236) notes that although the legal texts exist to protect foreigners from discrimination, Japan has fallen down in terms of "application and enforcement."

[40]As in many other advanced industrial societies, Japanese labor law does not distinguish among workers with regard to the applicability of labor standards and rights. *In practice*, however, violations of these standards and rights by unscrupulous employers often go unreported because of the foreign workers' clandestine status.

because typical workdays in the sectors in which unauthorized foreigners find employment can last more than eleven hours (Hormats et al. 1993, 70). Some workers have also reported cases of employers refusing to pay any wages at all.

In addition, while job-related injuries have increased (immigrants working "3K" jobs are at particular risk for injury), medical protections are scarce. Official reports show that the number of accidents involving unauthorized immigrants has risen significantly since the mid-1980s, but Japanese labor activists report that most of these accidents go unreported and, presumably, untreated. Many unauthorized workers apparently choose to remain silent rather than risk deportation or endanger the jobs of their foreign coworkers (Silverman 1992).

As with most states, the process of developing a public consciousness in Japan that stigmatizes unauthorized migration has been slow. However, as the number of unauthorized workers began to grow substantially, the debate about the issue became entangled with many other pressing social concerns. Kuwahara (1992, 2) writes that "the scope of the foreign labor 'problem' has since expanded (from issues of immigration control and employment) to 'social dimensions' and now involves all areas of life, including employment, housing, communities, work-related injuries, human rights, education and crime." As a result of this expansion, policy makers could no longer treat foreign workers as "invisible" or "disposable."

The abuse of unauthorized foreign workers has raised the profile of these workers even further. Kashiwazaki (1998, 242) notes that "a number of problems regarding citizenship rights arose in relation to the employment of migrant workers. They include labor accidents and medical care, breach in employment contracts, and the infringement of human rights in the sex industry." With increasing demands that foreign workers be treated in accordance with international conventions on human rights, the very existence of abuses within Japan came to be viewed in some quarters as evidence that immigration channels should be narrowed rather than expanded (Kashiwazaki 1998, 244).

The effort to regulate the flow and the working and living conditions of foreign workers goes back to the amendments to the Japanese Immigration Control Act that went into effect in June 1990. Up until that point, the government had hoped that "by pursuing the possibility of mobilizing the economically inactive population on the one hand, and by stimulating labor-curtailing measures, such as labor-saving investments and the redeployment of labor-intensive activities abroad, on the other, it could short-circuit the need for unskilled foreign labor" (Mori 1997, 95–96). Yet, neither technological innovation nor the amendments to the immigration act did much to reduce the demand for unskilled workers or stem their unauthorized migration into Japan. In fact, despite an explicit ban on unskilled foreigners and the drawing of a bright line between unauthorized and legal employment—making clandestine workers "institutionally non-existent" (Mori 1997, 189)—large numbers of both unskilled and clandestine workers continued to come to and find employment in Japan.

As noted earlier, the legislation broadened the categories under which temporary visas are issued and under which foreigners entering Japan are permitted to work. In fact, in many ways, the law brought Japan's temporary immigration practice in line with that of most other advanced industrial societies. In reluctant recognition of its new obligations as an economic superpower, and in an attempt to safeguard existing and secure new reciprocal opportunities for access to other countries for its own nationals, Japan expanded the number of job categories for which it would accept foreign workers (usually for three-year periods) to include the fields of teaching, law, banking, and accounting (Japan Ministry of Justice 1992, annex 18–20; Morita and Sassen 1994, 161). In addition, foreign students were authorized to work part-time so long as their jobs did not interfere with their academic progress. In most instances, before a foreigner could be employed, the prospective employer was obligated to demonstrate to the satisfaction of the labor authorities that the particular skill the foreigner possessed could not be found among available Japanese workers (Spencer 1992, 763), a labor market test commonly used by advanced industrial societies (Papademetriou and Yale-Loehr 1996).

Another significant provision of the 1990 law was the systematic admission of *Nikkeijin*, or descendants of Japanese emigrants, as a means of expanding the labor pool in a controlled and culturally "safe" fashion—as well as a means of substituting legal, ethnic Japanese for clandestine, non-Japanese Asians already working in the secondary labor market. Under the legislation, returning *Nikkeijin* were granted rights of employment and residence for an initial period up to three years (Spencer 1992, 762).[41] By 1998, estimates by the Japanese government put the number of *Nikkeijin* legally employed in Japan at 220,844 (SOPEMI, 1999a, 35).

Latin Americans of Japanese descent took advantage of the new legal opening. With the help of a protracted economic downturn in Latin America and rather extensive recruitment efforts, the number of migrants of Japanese descent from Latin America increased rapidly. Table 4 shows that the number of immigrants from South America increased from 3,961 in 1986 to 274,442 in 1998. Peruvians and Brazilians now account for 18 percent of the registered foreign population and 18 percent of the permanent resident population. Although these figures do not represent solely *Nikkeijin*, they certainly compose the overwhelming majority of South American immigrants to Japan.

The 1990 immigration amendments also barred entry to unskilled foreign workers and introduced severe penalties— including heavy fines and imprisonment—for agents who recruit and employers who hire clandestine workers.[42] In contrast to standard international practice at the time, the 1990 law allows not only deportation but also fines and imprisonment for apprehended unauthorized workers—provisions that Japanese authorities have been exercising with abandon, especially as unemployment rates increased in the second half of the 1990s (Iguchi 1999). A joint committee of the Ministries of Labor and Justice and the National Police Agency was set up to coordinate and bolster these efforts (Karasaki 2000).[43] In February 2000, Japan enacted even stronger regulations against unauthorized immigrants, raising the one-year ban on reentry to five years. The new rules also include fines or

---

[41]The treatment of *Nikkeijin* apparently leaves much to be desired. Numerous instances of housing and job discrimination against *Nikkeijin* have been reported (Oka 1994, 43–44). In fact, in his study of Brazilians in Nagoya, Japan, Jason Fox (1999) found that non-*Nikkeijin* Brazilians were often able to obtain higher-paying employment than their *Nikkeijin* counterparts. The non-*Nikkeijin* Brazilians' exotic looks enabled them to work in nightclubs and bars, which often paid more and required shorter hours than the factory work that most *Nikkeijin* obtained.

[42]Sanctions against employers reflect laws enacted by several Western European countries since the mid-1970s and by the United States since 1986 (Papademetriou 1993).

[43]In the first four years that the measure was in place, from 1990 to 1994, nearly 1,500 employers were arrested (SOPEMI 1994, 6).

TABLE 4.
Foreigners in Japan by Region of Origin, Nationality, and Permanent Resident Status, 1986 and 1998

Nationality	1986				1998			
	Number			% of Permanent Residents		Number		% of Permanent Residents
	Total	Permanent Residents	Others		Total	Permanent Residents	Others	
All nationalities	867,237	655,696	211,541	100.0	1,512,116	632,979	879,137	100.0
Asia	802,909	651,317	151,592	92.6	1,123,409	615,512	507,897	74.3
Koreas	677,959	627,423	50,536	78.2	638,828	559,065	79,763	42.2
China	84,397	22,757	61,640	9.7	272,230	36,995	235,235	18.0
Philippines	18,897	292	18,605	2.2	105,308	288	105,020	7.0
Thailand	2,981	67	2,914	0.3	23,562	235	23,327	1.6
Vietnam	4,388	78	4,310	0.5	13,505	3,332	10,173	0.9
Malaysia	2,182	73	2,109	0.3	6,599	353	6,246	0.4
India	2,601	312	2,289	0.3	8,658	834	7,824	0.6
Indonesia	1,839	51	1,788	0.2	14,962	300	14,662	1.0
Bangladesh	1,183	8	1,175	0.1	6,422	102	6,320	0.4
Pakistan	1,244	47	1,197	0.1	6,005	75	5,930	0.4
North America	34,235	1,644	32,591	3.9	54,700	5,585	49,115	3.6
United States	30,695	1,484	29,211	3.5	42,774	4,858	37,916	2.8
Canada	2,685	131	2,554	0.3	9,033	459	8,574	0.6
South America	3,961	106	3,855	0.5	274,442	6,738	267,704	18.1
Europe	20,500	1,775	18,725	2.4	39,925	3,951	35,974	2.6
United Kingdom	7,426	1,679	5,747	0.9	14,762	1,264	13,498	1.0
Germany	3,281	392	2,889	0.4	4,066	665	3,401	0.3
France	2,494	226	2,268	0.3	4,528	526	4,002	0.3
Other	5,632	854	4,778	0.6	12,027	932	11,095	0.8
Australia	2,058	65	1,993	0.2	7,613	261	7,352	0.5

Source: Ministry of Justice, Zairyu Gaikokujin Tokei, 1998 [Statistics on Registered Foreigners, 1998] (Tokyo: Ministry of Justice, 1999).

imprisonment for those who enter the country illegally (Tolbert 2000a).[44]

Tougher enforcement efforts, combined with the economic crisis, have led to only modest decreases in unauthorized migration (SOPEMI 1999b, 166). And any decrease has been more than offset by the increase in legal unskilled workers—namely, *Nikkeijin* and trainees.

The trainee program deserves particular mention. Under it, small and medium-sized Japanese firms without an overseas presence are given permission to hire unskilled foreign workers under the category of "trainees" in a particular job skill. Most firms recruit trainees through intermediary organizations such as employers associations, which exempts them from a 5 percent ceiling on the proportion of trainees to regular workers (SOPEMI 1999b, 167). Officially portrayed as an enlightened attempt to transfer skills and expertise to Japan's less-developed neighbors—which in some ways it does—the program brings in workers from other Asian countries to receive on-the-job training, Japanese language education, and formal classroom instruction for up to two years (Stahl 1992, 31).

According to the Ministry of Justice, 27,108 people officially entered Japan as trainees in 1998.[45] Of these, Chinese workers accounted for the largest share at 57.7 percent, followed by Indonesians (13.7 percent) and Filipinos (7.8 percent). The trainee program also includes a Technical Internship Training Program, which allows trainees who have passed special skills tests to change their status to "designated activities" and thereby acquire the same labor rights as Japanese workers. Technical interns are allowed to work for a maximum of three years (SOPEMI 1999b, 167). The number of technical interns has been growing rapidly since the beginning of the program in 1993 (see Figure 9), despite the highest unemployment rates in Japan in a generation.

---

[44] In the weeks before the enactment of the new regulations, the Japanese government issued over 13,000 permits for voluntary deportation to immigrants wanting to leave the country to avoid being caught under the new rules (Tolbert 2000a).

[45] It should be noted that this figure represents the number of trainees who are registered with the Japanese government (that is, those who have been in Japan for longer than ninety days). The number of entrants is actually much higher. In 1998, the government recorded close to 50,000 entries of trainees (SOPEMI 1999a, 21).

FIGURE 9.
Trainee Population and Status Adjustments, 1993–98

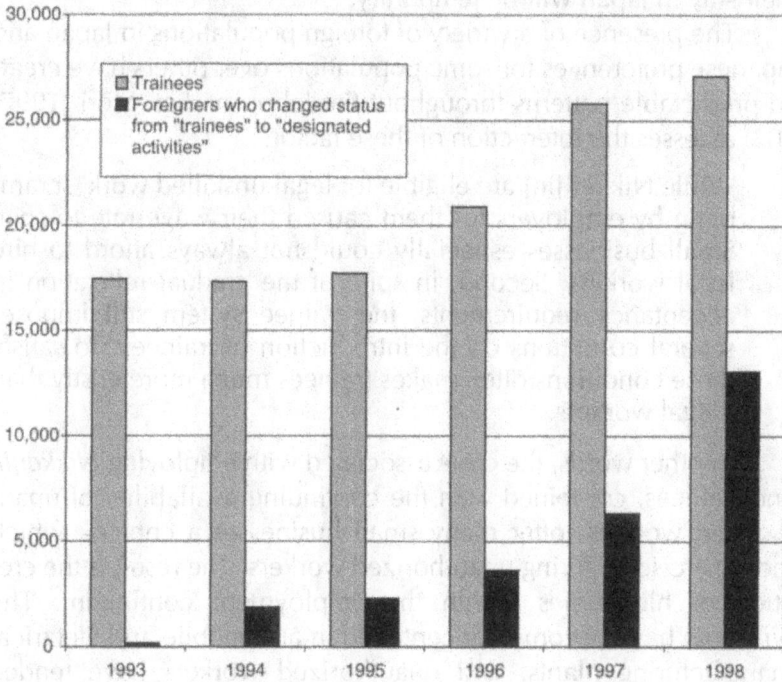

Sources: Japanese Immigration Bureau, Ministry of Justice; and Yasushi Iguchi, "Developments in the Japanese Economy and Their Impacts on the Labour Market and Migration," in Labour Migration and the Recent Financial Crisis in Asia (Paris: OECD, 1999).

Like the *Nikkeijin*, those participating in the training programs are heavily concentrated in the manufacturing sector and are employed in smaller firms. Where these two groups differ, however, is in their demographic profiles. Ethnic Japanese tend to immigrate with their spouses, their children, and sometimes even their parents, who left Japan decades ago (Oka 1994, 42). Furthermore, the 1990 legislation allows *Nikkeijin* to enter under long-term status. As Table 3 illustrates, 97 percent of Brazilians and 60 percent of Peruvians entered under a long-term provision, compared with only 27 percent of Chinese and 37 percent of Filipinos. Trainees, in contrast, are typically young males without family attachments. This difference highlights the essence of Japanese

41

policy to date: ethnic Japanese are allowed to bring their families and establish a sense of permanency, while Asian trainees must leave their relatives behind, thereby increasing the probability that their stay in Japan will be temporary.

The presence of a variety of foreign populations in Japan and Japanese preferences for some populations over others have created predictable patterns throughout the labor market. Mori (1997, 102) assesses the interaction of these factors:

> While Nikkei[jin] are eligible for legal unskilled work, scrambling by employers for them caused their wage rate to soar. Small businesses especially could not always afford to hire legal workers. Second, in spite of the gradual relaxation in acceptance requirements, the trainee system still imposes several conditions on the introduction of trainees. To satisfy these conditions often makes trainees much more costly than illegal workers.

In other words, the costs associated with employing *Nikkeijin* and trainees, combined with the continuing availability of unauthorized workers, offer many small businesses a choice—which they exercise by hiring unauthorized workers. The result is the creation of hierarchies within the employment continuum. The *Nikkeijin* have become concentrated in automobile and electrical manufacturing plants, and unauthorized workers have tended toward the construction sector, small urban manufacturing enterprises, and lower-tier service industries (Mori 1997, 174). Trainees, by far the smallest foreign worker cohort, are found in the low-wage sector. Thus, to a large extent, the 1990 immigration legislation provided the blueprint for the further segmentation of unauthorized and legal employment and, in many ways, for the ranking of lower-wage jobs on the basis of which cohort of foreigners is employed where.

Consistent with the experiences of virtually all other countries that have engaged in the foreign worker "game," including "traditional" immigration countries such as the United States, Canada, Australia, and New Zealand, more and more Japanese businesses have been relying on employment brokers to obtain foreign labor. Cornelius and Kuwahara document such use in Hamamatsu, where the "disposability" of *Nikkeijin* labor is "one of its most attractive qualities." They note: "Nikkeijin employed indirectly can be hired and returned to their brokers on short notice and without incurring any future obligations, damaging the company's image, or restricting future access to foreign workers" (1998, 36). Thus, the introduction of significant flexibility into the Japanese workforce through foreign labor is one of the main changes in the character of employment in Japan—and one that is already spreading to embrace native workers. At the same time, the use of brokers to access foreign workers signals that the employment of foreigners in the Japanese labor market is becoming institutionalized.

JAPAN AND ITS KOREAN COMMUNITY

All these large changes, and the many subtle ones that are not highlighted in this essay, should not be construed as changing the extreme skepticism of many Japanese about immigration. These changes are, however, fueling the debate about whether Japan will be able to break through the insularity and exceptionalism that have dominated both the Japanese self-image and others' image of Japan. Some of Japan's reluctance to engage the immigration issue head-on and in a progressive manner stems from its experience with its Korean minority. The continuing presence of Koreans in Japan challenges the dominant myth of ethnic homogeneity that still characterizes Japanese society's perception of itself. Japan's less-than-enthusiastic reaction to foreign workers is thus shaped in large part by its unresolved history with Koreans dating from 1910, when Japan colonized Korea.[46] The resulting disruption of Korean rural, agricultural communities gave way to increased migration to Japan. Typically, as Weiner (1994, 47) notes, "Koreans were expected to take up their 'proper place' within the empire; to accept a subordinate identity and serve the interests of Imperial Japan."[47]

---

[46]Migration relationships that trace their roots to imperial and colonial pasts are the hardest to erase, especially when strong political and economic relationships persist even after the imperial one wanes or disappears (Hamilton 1997). Japan's Korean minority is a case in point.

[47]Weiner argues that racial considerations strongly underpin the Japanese response to the Korean immigrant population. The dominant racial ideology, he argues, "conceived of the Korean as a member of a separate and inferior race and, when translated into a colonial environment, justified his continued subordination" (1994, 93).

By 1925, there were more than 136,000 Koreans residing in Japan; by the end of World War II, the number had grown to roughly 2 million. Although many Koreans returned home after the war, roughly 500,000 stayed behind as unskilled workers. Because they were displaced (by the now demobilized Japanese) and subsequently barred from sectors where they had once been employed in Japan, including construction and manufacturing, many of them turned to small enterprises.

In contrast to the multiethnic—if intolerant—Imperial Japan, post–War World II Japan turned toward increasing ethnic exclusivity. For a variety of social and political reasons, Koreans and Taiwanese in Japan have never been fully legally integrated. Kashiwazaki (1998, 145) goes further and argues that "Koreans have been the primary 'target group' concerning the regulation of Japanese state membership." The overlapping ideas of the common descent of all Japanese and of membership based on *jus sanguinis*, enshrined in Japan's 1950 nationality law, narrowed the membership options for the remaining foreign population in the country enormously. The exclusion, however, went deeper than this; "the postwar social disorder highlighted the differences between ethnic groups, while the independence of the Korean state reinforced the idea that the Koreans should belong to the peninsula" (Kashiwazaki 1998, 181).

In addition to the racial differences—emphasized in the political discourse about the place of the Korean minority in Japanese society—and Korea's independence following World War II, the manner in which Korean groups organized themselves in Japan (including their division into exclusively North or South Korean groups following the Korean War) contributed to their classification as outsiders. Demands for the conferral of certain rights for Koreans living in Japan as *foreign residents* rather than as Japanese nationals continued to distinguish and separate the ethnically Korean population from the Japanese and to constrain the possibility of their full incorporation.

As a percentage of total permanent residents in Japan, the Korean presence has decreased dramatically, from 78.2 percent to 42.2 percent between 1986 and 1998 (see Table 4). This shift confirms the growing diversity in immigrants that has come to characterize Japan. Nonetheless, Japan's current 678,000-member Korean minority still faces large-scale prejudice and discrimina-

44

tion. There have been repeated instances (including the famous Park case, which led to a landmark judicial decision in 1974)[48] of workers being dismissed when their Korean ethnicity was revealed. Until 1985, Korean permanent residents wishing to become citizens were, like other foreigners, forced to adopt a Japanese surname. Although a 1985 revision of Japanese national-ity law allowed foreigners to keep their surnames, an overwhelm-ing majority have adopted Japanese names as a practical necessity (Oka 1994, 15).

Another symbol of the Japanese government's uneasiness with its foreign population was the practice of fingerprinting for-eigners each time they renewed their registration cards, a proce-dure otherwise reserved for criminals. This practice was considered particularly offensive by Koreans, both because of their numbers and because many of them had been born and raised in Japan; they were "foreigners" in the eyes of the law but Japanese in almost all other respects. The application of the 1952 nationality law, and its underlying principle of *jus sanguinis*, made it difficult for second- and third-generation Koreans born in Japan to become citizens. The reaction to the practice eventually paid off: finger-printing was made a one-time-only requirement in 1987 and was finally abolished for most Korean legal permanent residents in 1992.[49]

Like the process of establishing permanent residency described earlier, the process of naturalization in Japan is not clearly defined, and the granting of citizenship is done on a case-by-case basis that can appear arbitrary. Either because of the diffi-culty of the process or because of a desire to maintain their Korean

---

[48]In 1970, Park Chong Sok, a nineteen-year-old Korean born and brought up in Japan, applied to a software plant owned by the Hitachi conglomerate using his Japanese name, Shoji Arai. He passed a stiff entrance exam and was accepted as an employee, only to be rejected when it was discovered that he was Korean. Park charged discrimination, demanded to be employed under his real name, and took the case to court. In 1974, a Yokohama court upheld his rights to employment and to use his real name. The landmark decision empowered other Koreans to follow Park's example, but it is estimated that 90 percent of Koreans in Japan continue to use their Japanese names (Oka 1994, 14–15).

[49] A large proportion of registered foreigners are still required to be fingerprinted. In 1999, 600,000 of the 1.5 million registered foreigners were fingerprinted. This policy may change soon, however; in March 1999, the Japanese Cabinet endorsed an amendment that would substitute a signature for a fingerprint when foreigners at least sixteen years old and living in Japan for more than twelve months register at local municipal offices (Globe Center 1999).

identity, many Koreans do not naturalize.[50] Instead, Koreans have spearheaded a movement to give permanent residents many of the rights of citizens. The right to vote is a key issue. Currently, permanent residents do not have the right to vote in elections, but that could change in the near future (Johnstone 1996). In 1995, the Supreme Court ruled that voting by foreigners is not unconstitutional but would be a matter for the Diet to consider. The Diet has begun to focus on the issue, with several opposition parties submitting voting-rights proposals. The ruling Liberal Democratic Party, however, has given only lukewarm support to the idea of granting voting rights to foreigners (Iitake 1999).[51]

JAPAN'S DOMESTIC POLICY DEBATE ABOUT FOREIGN WORKERS

Political and economic events since the mid-1970s may have had more of a transforming effect on Japanese society than is generally thought. Along with increasing opportunities for the admission of foreign workers, Japan has opened its markets to many foreign products and has become much more active internationally in matters beyond narrow economic and trade issues—including participating in international humanitarian initiatives and resettling Indochinese refugees following the end of the Vietnam War in 1975.[52] Acceptance of refugees has also meant signing and abiding by various international conventions that, among other things, prohibit certain forms of discrimination against noncitizen residents. Furthermore, the inevitable opening of its "cultural markets" to foreign, and especially American, culture has had an extraordinary influence on how Japanese youth perceives itself. When taken together, these changes may amount to the early

---

[50]About 15,000 people (9,700 of whom are Korean), or slightly more than 1 percent of the legally resident foreign-born population, are naturalized citizens (SOPEMI 1999b, 164, 265).

[51]There have been instances of Japan opening up to the political participation of foreigners in other ways. For instance, Marutei Tsurunen, a naturalized Japanese citizen originally from Finland, has run for public office in several elections. In 1998, he lost the election for a parliamentary seat in Kanagawa prefecture by only 7,000 votes. Tsurunen, an independent city assemblyman in Kanagawa since 1992, has capitalized on his foreign status, urging voters to "import a lawmaker direct from the land of Santa Claus" (Associated Press 1998).

[52]By 1991, roughly 8,000 Indochinese refugees had found a home in Japan (Kashiwazaki 1998, 237).

stages of a commitment to openness that will be difficult to arrest, let alone reverse.

The fact that foreign workers are already deeply embedded in the Japanese economy is borne out by their consistently large numbers throughout the 1990s, despite fifty-year highs in unemployment. The point has not been totally lost on the Japanese authorities, who have slowly begun to reexamine their traditional skepticism toward migration. Historically, the principal migration control and management bureaucracies—the Ministries of Justice and Labor—have been particularly cautious when it comes to immigration.[53] The collective tendency of these bureaucracies has been to view migration as a necessary evil to redress labor imbalances. This view accommodates limited short-term migration but is fundamentally hostile to permanent immigration. As a result, Japan's policies and their administration have reflected these bureaucracies' biases: namely, that Japan must not come to rely on foreign workers, and particularly not *unskilled* foreign workers, either as a legitimate response or as a permanent solution to its labor crisis.

The Ministry of Labor, especially, has argued that the admission of unskilled immigrant workers could lead to an avalanche of foreigners who, in turn, would undermine Japan's labor market and social cohesion. Among the adverse effects that the ministry has attributed to increased reliance on foreign workers have been the increasing stratification of the labor market along ethnic and immigration status lines and the unemployment of foreign workers in times of economic recession. Labor Ministry officials have also turned to a coterie of advisers in search of cost estimates to buttress arguments that as foreigners stay longer, and as their families join them, the social infrastructure costs will exceed the economic benefits they provide. Predictably, the ministry and its sotto voce allies found the necessary ammunition in the form of estimates

---

[53]It is important to note that other bureaucracies, most notably those concerned with foreign policy and trade, have been more sympathetic toward immigration. However, as is typically the case in advanced industrial societies, the issue has been narrowly defined as one of domestic policy and has thus been kept away from the bureaucracies with more broadly internationalist agendas. Although the Japanese penchant for consensus means that interagency competition may be less intense in Japan than elsewhere (at least after a decision is reached), adverse domestic reactions to immigration have continued to reinforce the position of domestic agencies over those involved with foreign affairs.

that purport to show that the social infrastructure costs of long-term immigration of low-skilled foreign workers and their families (such as wages for interpreters, housing costs, education costs, health and sanitation expenses, and so forth) would exceed the economic benefits of immigration (Oka 1994; Mori 1997).

The Ministry of Justice also marshaled an array of sometimes remarkably transparent objections to admitting unskilled foreign workers throughout most of the 1990s. These included the "expansion of domestic production" associated with their employment, "which contradicts efforts being made to reduce surplus, so as to correct the imbalance of trade between Japan and foreign countries and consequent increase of exports." The ministry also argued that admitting unskilled workers would hinder the economic development efforts of those workers' native countries, contending that workers' remittances would "be apt to result in non-productive consumption" (Japan Ministry of Justice 1992, 33–34).

Most restrictive official arguments—particularly those pointing to foreign workers as social burdens—have been at best incomplete, failing (really, refusing) to consider the full economic value of foreign workers. For instance, contrary to the Labor Ministry's concern about foreign workers creating labor market stratification, the Japanese labor market's segmentation is primarily the result of domestic social and economic policies and the realities of international competition. Foreign workers merely provide ailing and uncompetitive sectors with a fragile security, which in turn contributes to the health of the Japanese economy through both upstream and downstream economic effects. The concern about foreigners suffering from unemployment during economic downturns seems rather disingenuous. Evidence from elsewhere, as well as from the Japanese reality of the late 1990s, suggests that foreign labor may be even more valued during poor economic times.[54]

The economic case for immigration is even simpler to make. Japan has benefited greatly and disproportionately from the work of immigrants in "3K" jobs (benefits from the employment of better-skilled immigrants are even less in dispute). Without low-wage

---

[54]The issue becomes more complicated, however, when labor market inflexibility and regulation are high. Evidence from some European countries supports the Japanese position.

immigrant workers, the Japanese economy would have suffered tremendously, especially considering the low-wage sector's crucial place in the Japanese system of production. Japanese workers shun these marginal jobs, most of which cannot be exported without adverse upstream and downstream economic and labor market consequences; nor can they be technologically upgraded to the point where increasing productivity might allow "3K" firms to offer much better compensation packages (a prerequisite to better social standing). The Japanese thus have had little choice but to accept, however reluctantly, foreign workers. And if this syllogism reflects the relevant circumstances accurately, the proper policy decision—from an economic, social, and rights perspective— would be to accept such foreign workers through the main immigration gate and treat them properly.

The official positions of agencies of the Japanese government throughout the 1990s also failed to consider properly the other, less easily measured benefits of immigration, especially those associated with openness toward the outside world. These are benefits that Japan is likely to need as it begins to engage more fully with the international community. Although these benefits may appear to be subjective and thus less easily quantifiable, they can be decidedly positive. If foreigners are the only ones who will take some of the jobs available in Japan, then Japan may have to accept the burdens and challenges of the accompanying social, political, and cultural transformations that immigration entails, including the loss of its carefully tailored homogeneity.

Recently, however, some components of the Japanese government appear to be recognizing the inevitability of a change in policy and have begun to take some of the culturally prescribed steps necessary for initiating the serious internal discussions that must precede the reaching of a new consensus. In April 1999, Japan's Economic Council released a report titled "Considerations for the Japanese Socioeconomy in the 21st Century." The report recommended that "we should actively consider aiming to become a vibrant socioeconomy that is open to the world by orderly accepting migrant labor from overseas countries" in order to address future labor shortages, promote technology transfers to developing countries, promote Japanese culture, and contribute to "conceptual diversity and maintenance of market principles." A June 1999 report of the Globalization Committee of the Economic

Council expressed similar ideas with regard to the need for foreign workers, but it also made it clear that unskilled workers are not necessarily part of the equation. The report discussed unskilled foreign labor in the following deliberately vague language:

> The admittance of unskilled laborers and immigrants is expected to have a large effect on the Japanese socioeconomy and the lives of the Japanese people, as well as on the countries left by such immigrants and the immigrants themselves. For this reason, it is crucial to give careful consideration to this issue, starting with a consensus of Japanese citizens. From a long-term point of view, these issues should be discussed from a variety of perspectives.

In January 2000, the Prime Minister's Commission on Japan's Goals in the 21st Century released a report on governance in the new millennium. Arguing that Japan's focus over the next century should be on issues related to diversity, "global literacy," and individualism, the panel was particularly critical of Japan's historical conformity and group consensus over individual independence (Struck 2000). According to the report, to compete in the future and regain its sagging global stature, Japan should institute broad-ranging social changes, including adopting English as an official second language, reducing the school week, and *increasing immigration*. The report called for the creation of "a more explicit immigration and permanent residence system so as to encourage foreigners who can be expected to contribute to the development of Japanese society to move in and possibly take up permanent residence here."

And in fact, by the spring of 2000, the emerging shift toward greater openness to immigration was beginning to gain momentum. Even before the January 2000 report was released, the Ministry of Justice had called on Japanese to "aggressively carry out the smooth acceptance" of foreigners (French 2000c). And in March 2000, the Ministry of Justice announced plans to look into increasing the admission of foreign workers in response to the aging of Japanese society. The ministry will review long-term visa qualification requirements with an eye toward promoting greater immigration; it also plans to simplify procedures and expand the scope of the trainee program (*Yomiuri Shimbun* 2000).

One should not expect, however, any backtracking from aggressive support for policies designed to reduce the need for foreign labor. The government's public approach to labor shortfalls to date has been consistent with its overall approach to other economic and related matters before they reach the point of crisis—to stay the course but attempt to do better at it. Specifically, it has encouraged employers to offset labor shortages by improving efficiency and using labor-saving production techniques to the fullest. In addition to trying to attract more women and elderly to the workforce, proposals have continued to exalt such Japanese productivity mainstays as increased mechanization, standardization of parts, and the use of robots in production and construction. In addition, Japan's traditionally generous customer service guarantees have been reviewed in response to demands that the service sector make more efficient use of labor.

Other efforts have focused on decentralizing power in the administration and planning sectors and reforming the formal labor market. For instance, since the mid-1990s, the Ministry of Labor has encouraged the adoption of the five-day workweek, as well as the taking of paid annual leave (Japan Ministry of Labor 1994, 48). The rationale for these and similar initiatives is consistent with the ministry's traditional viewpoint—namely, that Japan's labor dilemma is primarily due to general mismatches in the labor market (rather than an absolute shortfall of workers) and can be addressed through what are by now "traditional" Japanese policy interventions.

However, while the government debate about foreign workers is gradually shifting toward a more open stance, the public debate, stoked by years of aggressive government rhetoric warning against a reliance on foreign workers, continues to be strongly anti-immigrant. Not surprisingly, opinion surveys have shown that most Japanese continue to oppose the admission of foreign workers. In fact, opponents of immigration continue to question immigration not only on economic grounds but also on the grounds of the social consequences of increased immigration. As one social critic wrote, "If . . . [Japan] formally decided on the introduction of foreign labor, it would receive immigrants from between 50 and 60 countries, and would be bound to become a multiracial society just like the United States" (Nishio 1992). This line of argument is calibrated to—and does—raise fears that immigration will lead to racial ghettos, rabid discrimination, and hate crimes on an unpredictable scale. And racism is also an important element of

51

anti-immigrant arguments in Japan, as it is elsewhere. Remarks like those of the governor of Tokyo, who said that "time and again, 'sangokujin' and foreigners committed atrocious crimes,"[55] make this all too clear (Sims 2000b).

FOREIGN DIRECT INVESTMENT AND OVERSEAS DEVELOPMENT ASSISTANCE

As noted earlier, Japan's efforts to address its labor dilemma have explored the possibility of "exporting" jobs through its extensive foreign direct investment (FDI) and overseas development assistance (ODA) initiatives. Such "deindustrialization," or "hollowing out," of the Japanese manufacturing sector has been relied on in part to reduce the need for manual labor in Japan (Cornelius and Kuwahara 1998, 2). Whether it can do so deeply enough to control the appetite for foreign workers once the Japanese economy recovers and its workforce shrinks even further will be fascinating to watch.

Japan's FDI and ODA have increased significantly since the mid-1980s as part of a strategy designed to take advantage of the strong yen (which made investments abroad cheaper) in order to create and capture emerging markets for Japanese goods produced at a substantial discount because of much lower labor costs (see Figure 10). Simultaneously, FDI has assumed the crucial role of "inoculating" Japan against protectionist quotas on Japanese products, especially in the developed world, where most Japanese direct investments have gone (see Figure 11). As Sassen points out (1998, 59–60), by 1990, Japan "had surpassed most of the leading Western European capital exporters, including Germany, the Netherlands, and France." Japan's capital presence in Asia in particular, along with its major influence through FDI, has increased dramatically as a result, making it the "single largest donor in China, Thailand, Philippines, Indonesia, and Malaysia" (Sassen 1998, 60) (see Figure 12). In fact, since 1992, a significant

---

[55]"Sangokujin" is a sharply derogatory term that literally means people from third countries. The governor also stated that foreigners could be expected to riot in the event of a disastrous earthquake. This statement is particularly inflammatory, because after the 1923 earthquake in Tokyo, Korean residents were massacred by Japanese who blamed them for setting fires and looting (Sims 2000b).

FIGURE 10.
Japanese Foreign Direct Investment and the
Strength of the Yen, 1980–98

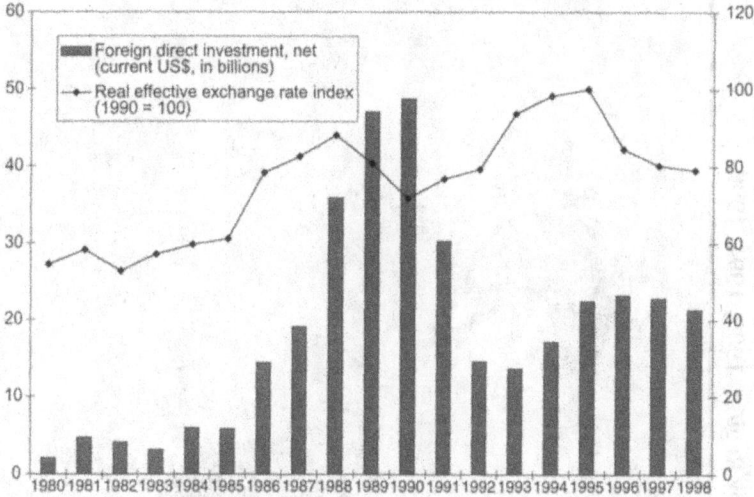

Source: World Bank, World Development Indicators 1999.

chunk—nearly half—of Japan's total FDI[56] has gone to Association of Southeast Asian Nations (ASEAN) countries[57] (see Figure 13).

As one would expect, Japan's principal aims in transferring labor-intensive industry to developing countries abroad have been to create (1) robust profit centers in countries eager for Japanese manufactures and (2) additional export platforms. During the Heisei boom, such transfers also had the advantage of relieving labor shortages in Japan. By the early 1990s, however, some in governmental and intellectual circles began to portray this practice as a purposely enlightened policy for addressing the pull and push factors that undergird much labor migration—by reducing the number of jobs in Japan (thereby reducing the job "magnet" for

---

[56]Japanese FDI in Asia rose steadily from 1993 to 1997 but dropped dramatically in 1998 after the onset of the economic crisis in the region.

[57]The member states of ASEAN are Brunei, Indonesia, Laos, Malaysia, Myanmar, Philippines, Singapore, Thailand, and Vietnam.

FIGURE 11.

Japanese Foreign Direct Investment by Region, 1989, 1994, 1998

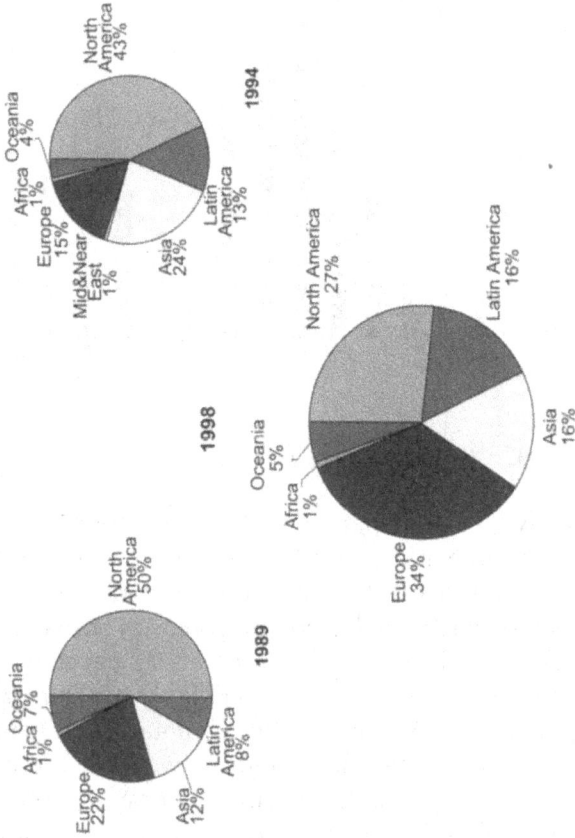

Note: Due to rounding, percents may not total 100.

Source: International Finance Division, Japanese Ministry of Finance.

FIGURE 12.
Japanese Foreign Direct Investment in
Asia by Country, 1989–98

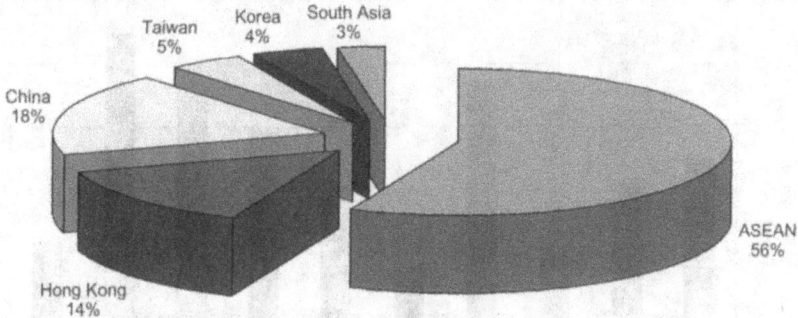

Note: ASEAN comprises the following countries: Brunei, Indonesia, Laos, Malaysia, Myanmar, Philippines, Singapore, Thailand, and Vietnam. South Asia includes India, Pakistan, Bangladesh, and Sri Lanka. Countries not included in the chart accounted for less than 1 percent of foreign direct investment.

Source: International Finance Division, Japanese Ministry of Finance.

unauthorized immigrants) and by contributing to large-scale job creation in prospective sending countries (thereby mitigating labor-expulsive forces in them) (see especially SOPEMI 1993, 62; Iguchi and Koike 1993). The estimated 1.6 million jobs created in Asia by Japanese FDI clearly added some credibility to this argument, despite its post hoc character (SOPEMI 1999a, 21).

However, such partly fortuitous migration-stemming and development-enhancing aspects of FDI and ODA—for example, mitigation of the effects of a restricted labor supply in Japan, creation of substantial employment opportunities abroad, and technology transfers to developing countries—have had an additional and somewhat perverse effect: they have created new (and strengthened preexisting) links between Japan and other countries in the region, which have in turn encouraged the formation of permanent transnational pathways from the countries receiving Japanese FDI and ODA to Japan. These pathways have predictably been exploited by immigrants from this same group of countries, who have sought entry and employment in Japan's transforming economy. As Sassen (1998, 74) points out, "internationalization

55

FIGURE 13.
Japanese Foreign Direct Investment in Asia and ASEAN
(in 100 millions of yen), 1989–98

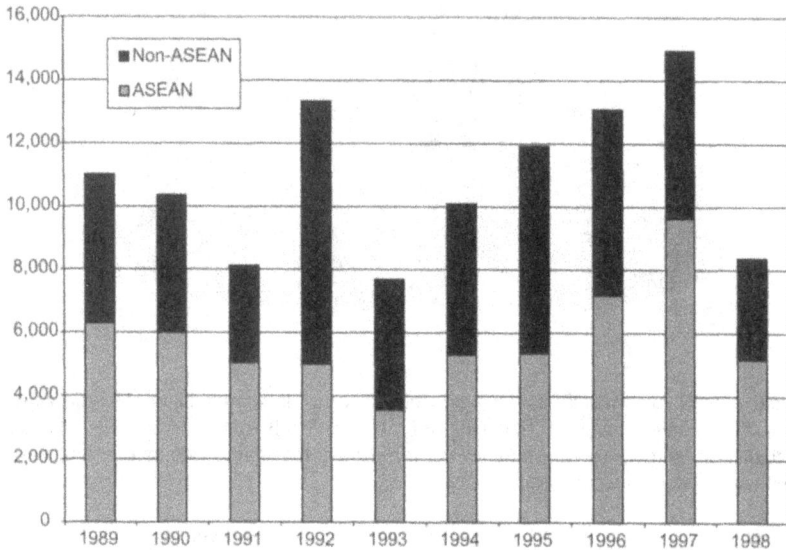

Source: International Finance Division, Japanese Ministry of Finance.

not only provides a context within which bridges are built with the countries of origin of potential emigrants, but also contributes to the Japanese economy becoming more porous, particularly in large cities."[58]

Japanese efforts to transfer production jobs abroad had several benefits. Yet there are limitations associated with this practice, besides those mentioned earlier that officials of the Japanese government have been slow to acknowledge. "While transferring [jobs] abroad is one way of dealing with domestic labor shortages," writes Charles Stahl (1992, 40), "the extent to which it can be a general solution to the problem is circumscribed by the immobility of capital in many of the industries affected by labor

---

[58]Sassen (1998, 70) argues that as Japan's international presence and aspirations grow, "it is likely to create—wittingly or not—transnational spaces for the circulation of goods, capital, and culture, which in turn may create conditions for the circulation of people."

56

shortages." As discussed earlier, the small and medium-sized firms, which collectively accounted for two-thirds of Japan's economic output (Shirouzu and Williams 1995), have struggled most with the worker deficit. However, it is overwhelmingly Japan's export sector—and within it, the larger and more successful Japanese firms—that has the capability to expand abroad. As the *Economist* pointed out, Japan's myriad small companies simply cannot afford to build factories overseas (1995, 23).

It is also clear that the notion that ODA and FDI will curb emigration pressures sufficiently to reduce unauthorized migration from Japan's less affluent neighbors in the Pacific in the short to medium term is little more than wishful thinking. This experience conforms with the academic literature on this topic, which raises reservations about the value of this approach in anything but the long run (Asencio Commission 1990). In addition, such efforts, even if theoretically successful in the longer term, cannot address migration pressures from farther afield; nor are they likely to have much effect on the decisions of those relatively skilled migrants who are seeking to improve their life chances by going abroad (UN Conference on Trade and Development 1994, 5). For instance, many of the unauthorized immigrants and most of the trainees who have made their way to Japan are relatively well educated individuals who can earn more in Japan as low-wage workers or factory trainees than they can as skilled workers in their own countries.

Perversely, again, FDI may actually narrow the range of opportunities for these individuals and therefore increase pressure on them to migrate, especially because Japanese overseas subsidiaries typically employ Japanese personnel for higher-level technical and administrative work (Conference on International Manpower Flows 1991, 16). So, while Japan closes its doors to "unskilled" foreign labor, many skilled positions abroad are typically filled by Japanese nationals. In short, it is unlikely that Japanese investment and development assistance abroad will ever come close to being a *sufficient* response to the dynamics of migration, and they can never be substitutes for sound economic and social policies that align themselves with, not against, the market. In fact, it is more likely that Japan's involvement in the Asian region will facilitate and deepen incipient ethnic pathways into Japan's domestic economy.

CONCLUSION

How close Japan is to a "third opening," that is, to a set of fundamental changes that match the transformations of the Meiji Restoration and of the post–World War II period, may still be a matter of disagreement. And the electoral setback of the Liberal Democratic Party (LDP), Japan's governing party, on June 25, 2000, will fuel such disagreements both within and outside Japan.[59] Certainly, de facto changes have been taking root in Japan. In fact, few doubt that greater engagement with the international community, broadly defined, has become institutionalized enough to be irreversible. However, much greater openness on the issues examined in this essay cannot be treated as "preordained" without concomitant deep changes in other realms. Among them are the restructuring of Japan's domestically focused production systems and their associated labor markets; the rejiggling of Japan's bureaucracy-dominated, consensus-based decision making; and deep reforms of the party system. Such developments, if they establish themselves as key societal goals,

---

[59]As this manuscript went to press, the LDP had lost its absolute majority (going from 271 to 233 seats), although it retained control of the Diet, the lower house, with the help of its two coalition partners. The main opposition party, the Democratic Party, which had campaigned on a platform espousing the need for such painful policies as higher taxes for all Japanese on top of spending cuts, experienced electoral gains of 32 seats, from 95 to 127 (see French 2000a). Some observers perceive the promise, or at least the possibility, of deep political change, as the election results suggest that the ruling coalition's lifeline has been shortened enormously. According to this view, the next couple of years are likely to be ones of transition—a period during which the forces of the sort of changes advocated in this essay prepare to take Japan forward (French 2000b). Others, however, most notably the *Economist*, interpret the election results as a continuation of the policy of "wait and hope" of the last ten years, which, in the magazine's analysis, leaves "Japan terribly vulnerable to another shock" (2000b, 22).

can release the Japanese economy and society from the grip of a plodding bureaucratic culture, move Japan toward a level of international involvement that is commensurate with its economic power (and responsibilities), and begin to create room for greater receptivity to ideas and people from other cultures. How Japan can achieve at least a working consensus on these goals and devise the necessary strategies to implement them remains unanswered.

Given Japan's repeated demonstrations of an uncanny ability to adapt to powerful forces that become irresistible, one might expect the Japanese government to be engaging in a crash course of sociocultural and political preparation proportionate to the gravity of the challenge. On the face of it, however, apart from a few government reports (such as those of the Economic Council) that outline in rather vague terms the need for social change, no *systematic* effort can be discerned. In this regard, how Japan handles the issue of immigration in the next few years may be a valuable proxy and weather vane for Japan's readiness to make truly fundamental changes. The immigration issue is multidimensional—intertwined with cultural, social, and economic factors—and thus requires unusual amounts of political leadership. The question is whether and how Japan might once again allow economic rationality and the country's clear interest in remaining the leading power in its region to dictate its policies toward immigration. This makes immigration one of the most interesting issues for Japan watchers to follow closely. The possibility that Japan might fail to seize the opportunity immigration represents only adds to its importance.

Japan's response will also be watched closely for ideas about how to address economic, and particularly demographic, imperatives with decisions about immigration. Some observers expect Japan, somehow, to be fleet-footed enough to avoid what they view as the false logic of the European guest worker experiments of the 1960s and 1970s (which allowed temporary immigration to become permanent immigration). Recent changes in laws governing the admission and treatment of foreigners suggest that Japan may be preparing to accept a certain amount of immigration-led diversification in its society. But will Japan be able to devise and stay the course of policies that increase its access to much-needed labor in certain sectors without backing into an unwanted permanent immigration program, with its attendant social and cultural consequences?

The labor market has posed and will continue to pose some of the biggest challenges to Japanese policy makers. There are several parts to Japan's labor market predicaments and the debate surrounding their resolution. The first part is the severe skill mismatches that are evident in every fast-changing economy. Specifically, as the economy changes, workers who are not able to keep up with the technical and knowledge content of their jobs become redundant (and thus expendable) at the same time that jobs requiring new skills remain unfilled. Although, in theory, a commitment to lifelong training can palliate *some* of that mismatch, the process of change is often too dynamic to hope for any substantial equilibrium.

The second part of Japan's labor dilemma stems from systemwide failures. Among them is Japan's apparent resistance to restructuring itself in ways that promote the most efficient allocations of capital and governmental goods and encourage and reward productivity. Restructuring would not only make Japan's economy more competitive; it would also create a possible template and lay the groundwork for the many more tough decisions needed to achieve continued prosperity.[60]

The third part involves decisions that fall under the rather sterile rubric of "rationalizing" the Japanese workforce further. Japan is not without its own pools of underutilized labor. For instance, unemployment rates among Japan's youngest and oldest workers are typically much higher than average unemployment rates and, not surprisingly, have been rising. In late 1998, with overall unemployment at 4.3 percent (it has since gone closer to 5 percent), those aged fifteen to twenty-four had an unemployment rate of 7.7 percent, and those between sixty and sixty-four had a rate of 10.9 percent.

---

[60]In the *Economist's* sharp and clearly impatient language, "[t]he system that Japan perfected from the 1950s onward was designed for an industrial society in its early stages of economic development. It is totally unsuited to a post-industrial world" (2000a, 28). It is this "1950s style" in matters ranging from management and administration to the way mainstream institutions perceive of and carry out their responsibilities that may be in need of the most radical change if Japan is to negotiate successfully the challenges of the twenty-first century.

The incorporation of women into the labor market is another anomaly resulting in large part from cultural norms. The much greater participation of women in Japan's labor market presupposes a radical departure from what is still acceptable in Japan, particularly among the current generation of economic and political leaders. Although women make up 51 percent of the population, they accounted for only 41 percent of the labor force in 1998, and many worked only part-time: 37 percent of women in the labor force in 1998 worked 34 hours or less per week (Japan Statistics Bureau 1999a).

The incentives for women to enter the Japanese labor force are limited. Most women are kept on a separate, lower career track from men. In fact, in 1998, women accounted for only 2 percent of directors (heads of groups made up of more than twenty employees or two departments) and 3 percent of section managers (heads of groups including more than ten employees or more than two sections). Such patterns begin early; the average first salary for female university graduates was 186,300 yen, compared with 195,500 for their male counterparts (Japan Policy Planning and Research Department 1999). Not surprisingly, thousands of young Japanese women have been leaving Japan in search of employment in Hong Kong in recent years (Doi and Willenson 1998).

Women's traditional roles within the home also limit their full and equal incorporation into the labor market. As a recent *New York Times* article explained, women "are expected to be *shokuba no hana*, or flowers in the workplace, brightening up the office with their presence, marrying sometime during their 20's and leaving the workplace to become mothers and homemakers" (French 2000d). Furthermore, women who continue to work after they are married face the double burden of work and housekeeping. In 1996, married working women spent nearly fifty times the amount of time that their husbands did on housekeeping (Japan Statistics Bureau 1998).

Neither the Japanese government nor the private sector is demonstrating a commitment either to fundamental restructuring or to rationalizing the labor force as deeply as necessary—at least as far as low-value-added operations and their attendant low-wage labor markets are concerned. As noted, the measures that have been taken so far do not go beyond the now traditional Japanese steps of exploring the limits of labor-saving technologies, parts standardization, and transfer of additional production and assembly operations abroad.

To address the labor market anomalies (many of which are exacerbated by cultural norms) and the severe demographic deficits that are the major focus of this essay, Japan will have to develop a systematic way of obtaining and, as importantly, *incorporating*, immigrant labor. This means that Japan will have no choice but to address the issue of its social and cultural intolerance of foreigners, including returning ethnic Japanese.

The challenge of developing the appropriate strategies to incorporate or at least to guarantee the rights of the foreign workers and their families who are supporting critical Japanese economic sectors is immense in human rights, social rights, and economic terms. Failure to acknowledge the reality of its emerging ethnic pluralism will interfere with Japan's ability to develop policies that might allow larger proportions of its long-term foreign-born residents to naturalize. This is a juridical and symbolic act that is, in most instances, a prerequisite to the fuller integration of the foreign born and their children. To the extent that Japan can make sense of its increasing social, ethnic, and religious diversity—and develop its own model of pluralism—other Japanese policy objectives can only be strengthened.

Anxiety that Japan might become a socially and economically two-tiered society if immigration is allowed to proceed may have been overtaken by the events of the last two decades. Japan has already become a multiethnic society, although on a far smaller scale than its industrialized counterparts. And a two-tiered society is already emerging, with predictable consequences. It draws its roots from Japan's imperial history with Korea and other countries in Asia and is complicated by the special status of the *Nikkeijin*. It is further driven by capital flows and ethnic networks. Japan, today, is populated with both legal and unauthorized immigrants of both sexes and by generations of mostly Korean immigrant families that call Japan home.

There is little doubt that important Japanese sectors and institutions will continue to resist the reality of the growing diversity in Japanese society—however slow and gradual it might be. Yet in the past, Japan has demonstrated extraordinary flexibility in responding to change, with seemingly ironclad rigidities melting away at the last possible moment when faced with political and economic realities. It would thus be unwise to assume that Japan's current labor market and demographic challenges—and the immigrants' places within them—will not be overcome as well. But neither should the challenge be underestimated.

If Japan chooses to open itself up to more immigration, it will have to decide whether to follow the model of the Gulf States (and Singapore) or that of most advanced industrial societies in terms of how it treats its immigrants and how much it invests in their integration. The likely appeal of the Gulf States model is that those states have worked diligently to prevent temporary migration from turning into permanent settlement—and have been somewhat successful. They have done so by building a regulatory regime designed to maximize the process's economic benefits by minimizing the migrants' social participation and its associated costs. In fact, they have given their immigration authorities complete discretion in enforcing an often draconian set of rules—including the annual turnover of as many as 1 million migrants and virtually no access to permanent residence or citizenship—which the authorities have implemented with remarkable rigor.[61]

Japan will surely be tempted to emulate the Gulf States model of strongly discouraging settlement. It is our contention, however, that Japan will have neither the determination nor the political and economic stamina (nor be able to muster the requisite consensus) to do so. Furthermore, we do not believe that Japan can be as impervious to outside human rights pressure in the long run as either Singapore or the Gulf States have been. A more important force, however, may be demographic realities—particularly as they relate to the labor force—which will compel a dramatic reconsideration of any "no settlement" approaches in favor of highly selective (especially in terms of skills and ethnicity) permanent immigration strategies. Because Japan's demographic predicament is acute, it is likely to be among the first Asian countries to venture into such regionally uncharted waters.

---

[61]Some Egyptian as well as Indian and Pakistani settlement in the Gulf States has nonetheless been taking place in the last few years through intermarriage and the emergence of "settled communities" of well-established and successful foreign entrepreneurs. But such examples are not yet significant relative to the movement's overall volume (Massey et al. 1998; Papademetriou forthcoming).

What is certain is that Japan is changing. It is a country with enormous strengths that has reinvented itself several times. The challenge today is precisely the one underscored by Prime Minister Obuchi's Commission on Japan's Goals in the 21st Century: how to open up to the benefits of globalization while reining in the backlash that can be expected to accompany such sweeping cultural and economic transformations. Immigration is one of the pillars that will need to be relied on to uphold such a bold vision. Whether Japan is flexible enough and willing to resist conservative pressures to tinker around the edges of needed reforms is yet to be demonstrated. Nonetheless, it is our conclusion that Japan's progress down this road is now irreversible.

EPILOGUE: SEVEN IMMIGRATION POLICY "RULES" FOR JAPAN TO CONSIDER

When Japan is ready to take on the issue of immigration and begin to think seriously about constructing a progressive yet robustly conceived and rigorously implemented immigration policy, the following do's and don'ts—based on the experience of others—might offer good overall guidance.

1. Make a serious commitment to developing immigration rules that are transparent, measured, enforceable, and administered consistently. Rules should lead to fair and predictable outcomes for immigrants and their families, as well as their employers. Failure to do so breeds cynicism and contempt for the system and encourages a culture of "gaming" it.

2. Commit to removing the ideological blinders that many countries wear when it comes to fully understanding how the various labor markets operate and the role of immigration in them. Armed with the resulting clarity, Japan should develop and enforce labor market regulations that remove the advantages of substandard wages, and particularly inferior work standards, from decisions about the employment of foreign workers. To succeed, new labor market rules must be consonant with fundamental market principles; that is, they must eschew overregulation and unnecessary and ultimately unsuccessful intrusion into the marketplace. At the same time, they must make sense for Japan as a society in terms of human and social rights.

3. Make immigration rules that respond quickly and unambiguously to labor shortages, skill mismatches, and related labor market anomalies, thus reducing employer incentives to violate the immigration laws in order to remain in business. Fail-

ure to do so confronts even the best corporate citizens with a choice between two nearly equally unpalatable options.

4. Maintain a robust, consistent, and sustained effort of border controls, and make sure that the consequences for those who break the rules are certain and swift. Over time, such efforts convey the unambiguous message that a state is serious about this most basic sovereign prerogative.

5. Engage in a strong and systematic anti-smuggling effort. Such an effort requires the investment of as many resources (financial, technical, or diplomatic) as necessary to combat human smuggling everywhere along the continuum, from the recruitment of prospective migrants to their delivery to a final Japanese destination (typically, a Japanese employer). Japan must fully engage in the multilateral efforts now under way with regard to smuggling. In addition, it must develop and aggressively pursue bilateral and regional diplomatic initiatives designed to stem organized smuggling efforts; this is achieved through enhanced cooperation in and assistance with enforcement efforts designed to disrupt and dismantle smuggling operations before their human cargo reaches Japanese soil.

6. Ensure that foreign-born individuals and their families who are in Japan and participate in its labor market are protected as diligently and fairly as Japanese citizens. No advanced democratic society—particularly no *orderly* society—can afford to allow ethnic and immigration-status distinctions to become entrenched; if this happens, the fundamental goals of equity and respect for the law will be undermined.

7. Finally, come to terms with the reality that Japan's de facto pluralism implies both added responsibilities on the part of the government and new attitudes on the part of Japanese societal institutions and the Japanese people. Principal among them are persistent efforts to create level playing fields in the social and economic realms and a commitment to allow long-term foreign residents who play by the rules to become *full* members of Japanese society.

REFERENCES

Abella, Manolo, and Hiromi Mori. 1994. "Structural Change and Labor Migration in East Asia." Conference paper on file with author.

Abrahams, Paul. 1999. "Japanese Unemployment Hits Record." *Financial Times*, August 1.

Appleyard, R., and C. W. Stahl. 1993. "Summary and Overview." *International Migration—Special Issue: Japan and International Migration* 31.

Asahi News Service. 1992. "Japan Reluctant to Allow Unskilled Foreign Laborers into Country." May 27.

Asencio Commission (Commission for the Study of International Migration and Cooperative Economic Development). 1990. *Unauthorized Migration: An Economic Development Response*. Washington, D.C.

Associated Press. 1998. "Finnish-born Candidate Loses Narrowly in Japanese Election." *Seattle Times*, July 14. www.seattletimes.com/news/nation-world/html98/finn_071498.html

Business Week. 1997. "Two Japans." January 27.

Chandler, Clay, and Kathryn Tolbert. 2000. "In Japan, Reviving an Ailing Economy." *Washington Post*, January 3.

Conference on International Manpower Flows and Foreign Investment in the Asian Region. 1991. Conference Report. Tokyo and Honolulu: Nihon University and East-West Center Population Institute.

Cornelius, Wayne A. 1994. "Japan: The Illusion of Immigration Control." In *Controlling Immigration: A Global Perspective*. Edited by Wayne A. Cornelius et al. Stanford: Stanford University Press, 375–410.

Cornelius, Wayne A., with Yusuo Kuwahara. 1998. "The Role of Immigrant Labor in the U.S. and Japanese Economies: A Comparative Study of San Diego and Hamamatsu, Japan." Report for the Center for U.S.-Mexican Studies, University of California–Davis. April 1.

Doi, Ayako, and Kim Willenson. 1998. "The Birthrate and the Bust: How Career Choices and Fewer Babies Are Undermining Japan's Future." *Washington Post*, July 26.

Economist. 2000a. "After Japan's Election: Sunset for the Men in Suits." July 1.

———. 2000b. "Vulnerable Japan." July 1.

———. 1999. "Will Japan Ever Learn." November 6.

———. 1995. "A Question of Balance." April 22.

Fox, Jason. 1999. "Race, Ethnicity and Employment Patterns of Brazilian Immigrants in Nagoya, Japan." *Asian Migrant* 12 (October/December): 119–28.

French, Howard W. 2000a. "Japan's Governing Party Suffers Severe Election Setback." *New York Times*, June 26.

——. 2000b. "Signs of Life in Japan." *New York Times,* June 27.

——. 2000c. "Still Wary of Outsiders, Japan Expects Immigration Boom." *New York Times,* March 14.

——. 2000d. "Women Win a Battle, but Job Bias Still Rules Japan." *New York Times,* February 26.

Globe Center Legal Updates. 1999. "Japan: End to Fingerprinting?" Immigration in Asia: Japan (April). www.globecenter.com/news /Apr1999/japan.htm

Hamilton, Kimberly. 1997. "Europe, Africa, and International Migration: An Uncomfortable Triangle of Interests." *New Community* 23 (October 1997): 549–70.

Hanami, Tadashi. 1998. "Japanese Policies on the Rights and Benefits Granted to Foreign Workers, Residents, Refugees, and Illegals." In *Temporary Workers or Future Citizens?* Edited by M. Weiner and T. Hanami. New York: New York University Press, 211–37.

Harney, Alexandra. 1999. "Restructuring Gives Japan's Workers Culture Shock." *Financial Times,* November 2.

Hirsch, Michael, and E. Keith Henry. 1997. "The Unraveling of Japan, Inc." *Foreign Affairs* (April): 11–16.

Hormats, Robert, Doris Meissner, Shijuro Ogata, and Antonio Walker. 1993. *International Migration Challenges in a New Era: A Report to the Trilateral Commission.* New York, Paris, and Tokyo: Trilateral Commission.

Hoshiai, Yuriko, and Bill Powell. 1990. "Help Wanted." *Newsweek,* July 16.

Iguchi, Yasushi. 1999. "Illegal Migration, Overstay, and Illegal Working in Japan: Development of Policies and Their Evaluation." Room document for the OECD Seminar on Preventing and Combating the Employment of Foreigners in an Irregular Situation, The Hague, April 22–23.

Iguchi, Yasushi, and Osamu Koike. 1993. "International Labor Migration and Labor Market Policy in Japan." Conference paper on file with author.

Iitake, Koichi. 1999. "Diet Spotlight on Vote for Foreigners: Political Parties Warm to the Controversial Idea of Suffrage for Permanent-Resident Foreigners as a Way to Enhance Their Support Base." *Asahi Evening News,* November 2.

Japan Economic Council. 1999. *Report of the Globalization Committee.* www.epa.go.jp/99/e/19990629e-global-e.html

Japan Economic Council, Fundamental Concept Committee and Planning Committee. 1999. *Considerations for the Japanese Socioeconomy in the 21st Century.* April 13.

Japan Economic News Wire. 1996. "Home Minister Kurata Defends Nationality Clause." May 14.

Japan Immigration Association (JIA). 1995. *1994 Statistics on Immigration Control.* Tokyo: JIA.

———. 1998. *1997 Statistics on Immigration Control.* Tokyo: JIA.

———. 1999. *1998 Statistics on Immigration Control.* Tokyo: JIA.

Japan Local Government Center (JLGC). 1999. "Decentralization: New Legislation Boosts Japan's Local Authorities." *JLGC Newsletter* 31 (summer).

Japan Ministry of Justice. 1992. "Basic Plan for Immigration Control, Notification Number 319." Tokyo: Japan Immigration Association.

———. 1999. *1998 Statistics on Registered Foreigners.* Tokyo.

Japan Ministry of Labor. 1992. "Foreign Workers and Labor Market in Japan." Paper presented at IOM/APIC Conference on Japan and International Migration, Challenges and Opportunities, October 7–9.

———. 1994. *White Paper on Labor 1994: Tasks on Enriching Working Life Based on Stable Employment.* Tokyo: Japan Institute of Labor.

Japan Policy Planning and Research Department, Minister's Secretariat, Ministry of Labor. 1999. *Basic Survey on Wage Structure.* Tokyo.

Japan Press Weekly. 1999. "Struggle for Better Working Conditions." December 18.

Japan Statistics Bureau, Management and Coordination Agency. 1996. *1996 Japan Statistical Yearbook.* Tokyo.

———. 1998. *Survey on Time Use and Leisure Activities.* Tokyo.

———. 1999a. *Annual Report on the Labor Force Survey.* Tokyo.

———. 1999b. *1999 Japan Statistical Yearbook.* Tokyo.

Johnstone, Christopher B. 1996. *Japan's Foreign Residents and the Quest for Expanded Political Rights.* Japan Economic Institute Report, July 19.

Jones, Gareth. 1992. "Japan Faces Multi-Racial Challenge." *Reuter Library Report,* March 17.

Karasaki, Taro. 2000. "Ministries Pledge to Curb Illegal Workers." Asahi News Service, March 10.

Kashiwagi, Akiko, and Clay Chandler. 2000. "Japanese Parliament Approves Measure to Reform Pensions." *Washington Post,* March 29.

Kashiwazaki, Chikako. 1998. "Nationality and Citizenship in Japan: Stability and Change in Comparative Perspective." Doctoral thesis, Brown University.

Kuptsch, Christiane, and Nana Oishi. 1995. "Training Abroad: German and Japanese Schemes for Workers from Transition Economies or Developing Countries." International Migration Papers no. 3. Geneva: International Labor Office.

Kurtenbach, Elaine. 1992. Untitled article. Associated Press, August 16.

Kuwahara, Yasuo. 1992. "To Tie the Untied String: Migrant Workers and Japan's Economic Cooperation." Working Paper no. 70. Geneva: International Labor Office.

Kyodo News. 2000. "Number of Foreigners Staying Illegally in Japan Declines." March 31.

Mainichi Daily News. 1996a. "Kawasaki Scraps Nationality Clause for City Workers." May 14.

Mainichi Daily News. 1996b."Kawasaki's Step Forward." May 15.

Massey, Douglas S., et al. 1998. *Worlds in Motion: Understanding International Migration at the End of the Millennium.* New York: Oxford University Press.

Mori, Hiromi. 1997. *Immigration Policy and Foreign Workers in Japan.* New York: St. Martin's Press.

Morita, Kiriro, and Saskia Sassen. 1994. "The New Illegal Immigration in Japan 1980–1992." *International Migration Review* 28 (spring): 153–64.

Neff, Robert. 1992. "Japan: Will It Lose Its Competitive Edge?" *Business Week,* April 27.

Nishio, Kanji. 1992. "Some Believe Accepting Foreign Workers Could Lead to Corruption." *Japan Times Weekly—International Edition,* March 5–11.

Oka, Takashi. 1994. *Prying Open the Door: Foreign Workers in Japan.* Washington, D.C.: Carnegie Endowment for International Peace.

Organization for Economic Cooperation and Development (OECD). 1995–96. "Aging Populations and Government Budgets." *OECD Observer* 197 (December/January): 36.

Ozawa, Ichiro. 1996. "The Third Opening," *Economist,* March 9.

Papademetriou, Demetrios G. 1993. "Confronting the Challenge of Transnational Migration: Domestic and International Responses." In *The Challenge of South-to-North and East-to-West Migration.* Paris: OECD.

———. Forthcoming. *International Migration and U.S. Security Interests: An Overview and Assessment.* Washington, D.C.: Carnegie Endowment for International Peace.

Papademetriou, Demetrios G., and Stephen Yale-Loehr. 1996. *Balancing Interests: Rethinking U.S. Selection of Skilled Immigrants.* Washington, D.C.: Carnegie Endowment for International Peace.

Pei, Minxin. 1999. "Is China Stable?" *Asian Wall Street Journal,* July 28.

Peterson, Peter. 1999. "Gray Dawn: The Global Aging Crisis." *Foreign Affairs* 78 (January/February): 42–55.

Piquero-Ballescas, Ma. Rosario. 1998. "Migration of Filipino Women to Japan: Continuities and Shifts." *Asian Migrant* 11 (July/September): 83–88.

Prime Minister's Commission on Japan's Goals in the 21st Century. 2000. *The Frontier Within: Individual Empowerment and Better Governance in the New Millennium.* www.kantei.go.jp/jp/21century /report/overview.html

Sassen, Saskia. 1998. *Globalization and Its Discontents.* New York: New Press.

Shirouzu, Norihiko, and Michael Williams. 1995. "The Big Squeeze," *Wall Street Journal,* July 25.

Silverman, Gary. 1992. "A Life's Value: Japanese Court Raises Questions Worldwide on Rights of Illegal Immigrants in the Workplace." *Newsday,* July 19.

Sims, Calvin. 2000a. "Japan's Employers Are Giving Bonuses for Having Babies." *New York Times,* May 30.

———. 2000b. "Tokyo Chief Starts New Furor on Immigrants." *New York Times,* April 10.

SOPEMI (Système d'observation permanente des migrations), Organization for Economic Cooperation and Development. 1993. *Trends in International Migration.* Paris: OECD.

———. 1994. Annual internal report: Japan. Tokyo.

———. 1999a. Annual internal report: Japan. Paris, December.

———. 1999b. *Trends in International Migration.* Paris: OECD.

Spencer, Steven A. 1992. "Illegal Migrant Laborers in Japan." *International Migration Review* 26 (fall): 754–87.

Stahl, Charles W. 1992. "Asian International Labor Migration." Paper presented at Sixth National Conference of the Australian Population Association.

Struck, Doug. 2000. "Think American, Japanese Are Advised." *Washington Post,* January 20.

Struck, Doug, and Kathryn Tolbert. 2000. "Japan Inc. Workers Get Harsh Dose of Economic Reality. *Washington Post,* January 3.

Tett, Gillian. 1999. "Bank of Japan Acts on Job Cuts Advice." *Financial Times,* November 2.

Tolbert, Kathryn. 2000a. "Illegal Residents Rush out of Japan to Avoid Penalties." *Washington Post,* February 18.

———. 2000b. "Japan Opens a Door to Emigrant's Descendants." *Washington Post,* March 7.

Toriyama, Tadashi. 2000. "Discussion Vital over Plans to Accept Nursing-Care Workers from Overseas." *Daily Yomiuri,* April 26.

United Nations Conference on Trade and Development and International Organization for Migration. 1994. *Foreign Direct Investment, Trade and International Migration.*

United Nations Population Division, Department of Economic and Social Affairs. 1997. *World Fertility Patterns 1997.* ST/ESA/SER.A/165. New York: United Nations.

———. 2000. *Replacement Migration: Is It a Solution to Declining and Ageing Populations?* New York: United Nations.

Weiner, Michael. 1994. *Race and Migration in Imperial Japan.* New York: Routledge.

Wong, Simon. 2000. *Patterns of Internal Migration in China.* Washington, D.C.: Carnegie Endowment for International Peace, International Migration Policy Program.

WuDunn, Sheryl, and Nicholas D. Kristof. 1999. "Japan, a Land of Savers, Wallows in Public Debt." *International Herald Tribune,* September 2.

Yomiuri Shimbun. 2000. "Ministry Eyes Boosting Immigration." March 24.

Demetrios G. Papademetriou is a senior associate and the codirector of the International Migration Policy Program at the Carnegie Endowment for International Peace, where his work work focuses on (1) evaluating the adequacy of U.S. immigration and refugee policies and administrative structures and practices in meeting U.S. objectives, (2) the migration politics and policies of European and other advanced industrial societies, and (3) the role of multilateral institutions in developing and coordinating collective responses to international population movements. He is also the cofounder and international cochair of *Metropolis: An International Forum for Research and Policy on Migration and Cities.* Mr. Papademetriou has served as chair of the Migration Committee of the Paris-based Organization for Economic Cooperation and Development (OECD) and as director for Immigration Policy and Research at the U.S. Department of Labor, where he chaired the Secretary's Immigration Policy Task Force. Mr. Papademetriou has published widely on the immigration and refugee policies of the United States and other advanced industrial societies, the impact of legal and illegal immigration on the U.S. labor market, and the relationship between international migration and development. He received his Ph.D. in Political Science from the University of Maryland in 1976.

Kimberly A. Hamilton is senior international program officer at Alcoa Foundation. Prior to joining Alcoa Foundation, she was program officer at the Howard Gilman Foundation where she directed programs on global HIV/AIDS, environmental conservation, and humanitarian relief and human rights. She has also worked at the Center for Strategic and International Studies, first in the African studies program and later as associate director of international economic and social policy. Ms. Hamilton has written extensively on international migration and on the challenges of global HIV/AIDS. She holds a doctorate in demography from Brown University (1997) and a masters in international relations from the Johns Hopkins School of Advanced International Studies (1989). The views expressed in this volume are independent from her professional affiliations.

INTERNATIONAL MIGRATION
POLICY PROGRAM

The salience of international migration and the strong reactions it provokes have placed the issue at the center of political debates throughout the industrial world. Migration's multiple facets pose almost as many challenges as they present opportunities and have implications for different levels of government as well as society's constituent groups.

The Endowment's International Migration Policy Program is a leading source of expert analysis and policy ideas on migration and refugee issues. The Program focuses on bridging the worlds of research and policy in these areas, bringing an independent voice to migration and refugee policy debates here and abroad, and enhancing public understanding of these and related issues.

Program staff work with officials of numerous governments, leading independent institutions in the United States and abroad, and various United Nations and other international agencies. Among the latter are the Organization for Economic Cooperation and Development, the International Organization for Migration, and the UN High Commissioner for Refugees. The International Migration Policy Program's core activities are funded by the Ford Foundation, the John D. and Catherine T. MacArthur Foundation, and the Mellon Foundation.

CARNEGIE ENDOWMENT
FOR INTERNATIONAL PEACE

The Carnegie Endowment is a private, nonprofit organization dedicated to advancing cooperation between nations and promoting active international engagement by the United States. Founded in 1910, its work is nonpartisan and dedicated to achieving practical results. Through research, publishing, convening and, on occasion, creating new institutions and international networks, Endowment associates shape fresh policy approaches. Their interests span geographic regions and the relations between governments, business, international organizations, and civil society, focusing on the economic, political, and technological forces driving global change. Through its Carnegie Moscow Center, the Endowment helps to develop a tradition of public policy analysis in the states of the former Soviet Union and to improve relations between Russia and the United States. The Endowment publishes *Foreign Policy*, one of the world's leading journals of international politics and economics, which reaches readers in more than 120 countries and in several languages.

www.ingramcontent.com/pod-product-compliance
Lightning Source LLC
Chambersburg PA
CBHW011830020426
42334CB00027B/2999